MIND YOUR VISION:
2020 AND BEYOND

Mind Your Vision: 2020 and Beyond
Copyright © 2020 by
Rachel Latrell Moore and Moore of Rachel, Inc.

All rights reserved, including the right to reproduce this book or portions thereof in any form whatsoever, or stored in a retrieval system, or transmitted in any form or by any means electronic, mechanical, photocopied, recorded, or otherwise without express written permission of the author or publisher, except where permitted by law. All logos, artwork, designs, and instructions are protected under copyright law.

For permissions contact www.mooreofrachel.com;
rachel@mindyourvision.com

ISBN: 978-0-9975638-0-1

The information contained in this book is intended to be inspirational and educational.

Unless otherwise indicated, Scripture quotations are from The Holy Bible, English Standard Version ® (ESV®), (NIV®), or (KJV®), copyright © 2001 by Crossway, a publishing ministry of Good News Publishers. Used by permission. All rights reserved.

Printed in the U. S. A.

J-Star Publishing: www.mooreofrachel.com

Moore of Rachel Inc.

Editing and book interior design by Jean Boles
https://www.upwork.com/fl/jeanboles4

Book cover design by Tanya Viduya
https: //www.behance.net/tanyaviduya

Illustrations by Jeremy Moore : jeremy.moore5699@gmail.com

MIND YOUR VISION

2020 AND BEYOND

Transform Your Dreams and Goals into Reality

RACHEL MOORE
International Best Selling Author

I dedicate this book to my wonderful sons for their gracious contribution of time and talent toward the completion of this book. Within these pages, I share stories where our faith was stretched to believe for a desired outcome. Each story conceived through a decade of "Family Visioning" moments together ended so incredibly. Now is the time to share them with the world.

Contents

ACKNOWLEDGMENTS 9
PREFACE 11
    Note To You, Dear Reader: 11
INTRODUCTION 15
CHAPTER 1: FIND CLARITY 19
    Focus on What You Can Change 21
    Finding Clarity 22
    What's Clouding Your Vision? 24
CHAPTER 2: BRING YOUR LIFE IN FOCUS 27
    The Four Connection Quadrants 27
    Get Clarity within the Quadrants: 33
CHAPTER 3: APPLY FOCUS POWER 39
    Breaking down FOCUS 42
    Foundation of Focus 45
CHAPTER 4: WRITE THE VISION 49
    A Decade of Family Visioning 49
    Dream with Your Kids 51
    The Magic of Believing as a Family 53
    The Visioning Process 63
    What is Family Visioning? 65
CHAPTER 5: PREPARE TO CREATE 69
    The Top 10 Reasons Tote-a-Vision Will Change Your Life 74

CHAPTER 6: MASTER YOUR MINDSET 77
No Longer Resist the Possibilities 77
Mindset Matters 78

CHAPTER 7: DECLARE VICTORY 87
Declare Victory Over Battles in Your Mind 87
Declare Victory Over Adversity 93

CHAPTER 8: GROW IN WISDOM 97
The Wisdom Effect 97
Lessons of Four Little Things Upon the Earth
that are Exceedingly Wise 103

CHAPTER 9: POWER-UP YOUR DREAMS 107
Keys to Making Progress Toward Your Vision 107
Steps to Practicing Daily Visioning 108

CHAPTER 10: OWN IT AND CARRY-ON 117
Effective Ways to Endure Delays 122

CHAPTER 11: PURSUE PASSION, DISCOVER PURPOSE .. 129
Discover Purpose in the Process of Pursuing Passion 129
Four Ways to Find Hidden Potential 136
Develop Your Potential 138

CHAPTER 12: *FAITH IT* UNTIL YOU MAKE IT 141
The Principle of Faith 144
How Faith Works 145

CHAPTER 13: PREVAIL OVER DOUBT 153
Six Ways to Prevail Over Doubt 154

CHAPTER 14: PERSONIFY PERSISTENCE 163
Persistence Personified 163

Adversity Meets Persistence 171
CHAPTER 15: STEP OUT OF THE BOX 173
    Operating in the Faith Zone... 173
CHAPTER 16: INFLUENCE YOUR DESTINY 177
CHAPTER 17: JOURNAL TO SUCCESS................................ 187
    Write for Insight 188
    Take time for Reflection 191
    Different Types of Journals for Your Life Journey.......... 195
CHAPTER 18: APPLY MINDFUL METHODS 201
CHAPTER 19: BE INSPIRED TO ASPIRE 215
CHAPTER 20: BE SMART WITH YOUR GOALS 219
TESTIMONIALS FROM INDIVIDUALS WHO
ATTENDED *MIND YOUR VISION* SEMINARS: 223
CONCLUSION 227
RESOURCES...231
    Tote-a-Vision details:..231
    Benefits of Tote-a-Vision: 231
    "Manifest More" Audio Course:..................................... 232
    Podcasts: 232
WORKS CITED 233
ABOUT THE AUTHOR.. 235

Acknowledgments

Thanks to everyone on my book project team who helped me so much. Special thanks to Tanya, the wonderfully creative mind behind the cover design, to Jean Boles, the editor and incredible interior designer, to my son Jamicah, the clever cover-art photographer, and to my son Jeremy, the best illustrator I know.

Special thanks to my sons Jamicah and Jonathan for the amazing production of the book trailer video and envisioning film, and thanks to Tanya for doing such an outstanding job on designing such appealing book marketing materials.

PREFACE

Note To You, Dear Reader:

I encourage you to make manifesting your goals a journey and not a final destination. Find your place in this world to make a difference for the greater good, and then use your blessing to bless others.

It's important to note that through knowledge, understanding, and the application of knowledge you can achieve your goals, but that love, character, and integrity are what keep you in a place of true wealth and prosperity.

Many of the principles listed within this book are based upon a book of wisdom that I live by. Much of our success depends upon understanding the power within us and upon staying connected to a divine source greater than ourselves: God, the creator of the universe.

"As for every person God has given riches and wealth, and enables them to enjoy their possessions, to accept their portion and be happy in their work—this is a gift from God" (My paraphrase from Ecclesiastes 5:19).

Benefits of reading this book:
- Learn to no longer allow life to just happen; you will actively choose your course
- Set direction for your life to achieve your dreams

- Discover techniques to keep your mind focused and positive
- Gain clarity of vision for what you want in life
- Find action steps to take toward achieving your dreams
- Learn to create a Vision/Dream Board that reflects your hopes and dreams

This book will challenge you to:
- Think outside the box
- Be more optimistic
- Believe contrary to what you see in your current circumstances
- Stay focused
- Be disciplined
- Be organized
- Be proactive

These challenges are more easily conquered by some than others, but if you follow the steps in this book, you will progress and discover that all things are possible when you believe in possibilities.

Throughout this book, we will refer to your hopes, dreams, goals, or desires as your "IT."

Here are some of the points covered:
- Learn the process of family visioning
- Learn how to involve your children in the process
- Discover what's clouding your vision
- Learn how to be a person of pro-active faith
- Discover techniques to help keep you focused
- Learn how to speak affirmations and decrees over your life

- Create a personal, portable vision board with the Tote-a-Vision
- Learn keys to making progress toward your vision
- Learn to how to use the Tote-a-Vision journal to track your progress
- Learn how to incorporate financial goals to achieve your life vision

INTRODUCTION

On December 28, 2019, I awoke without the sound of an alarm. I was still enjoying my Christmas holiday staycation at home, so there was no need to hurry to start my day. As I lay resting in bed, a notification flashed on my phone, so I decided to check it out. It was a Facebook message. After reading the message, I scanned my Newsfeed and a post got my attention. I didn't recognize the person's name, but since one of my sons had "liked" the post, I assumed that it was someone whom they knew. The individual had posted a personal statement describing their seasonal depression, but felt it was even worse this time around. They were terrified with the tormenting thought that this emotional struggle would become their new norm. They wrote, "It's a daily struggle, I can barely pull myself out of bed." This post was a cry for help, and my heart heard it loud and clear. Then thoughts of my past experiences flooded my mind, such as almost accepting the pain from continuous muscle spasms being my norm, to almost accepting being told no as a final answer to my desire to make my kids' dreams come true. My heart was so touched by the Facebook post that I had to at least share a condensed version of what helped me become the victor in each situation.

I replied, "Try this technique. Refocus your thoughts on positive things. Start by writing down several things that you are grateful for in your life, such as, 'I am grateful for life, health, and strength. I am grateful for my family, I am grateful for….' Next, write down what you want to be, do, and have in your life. Refuse to focus on the 'how it will happen' right now. Focus on things that *you* can do and not on other people. You can't control what others do, but you can control your thoughts and actions. Just write down your desires. Then focus your thoughts on visualizing the possibilities. God wants to bless us with good things and with the desires of our hearts. Ask God to strengthen your faith to believe for those things to manifest in your life. It's your connection and anchor for 2020 Vision. What do you desire for your life in the coming year, 2020? Write down your vision and make it plain!"

As I was typing the message, I was reminded that my *Manager Mom: Mind Your Vision* book listed these mind-freeing techniques and more. I wrote that book from a mom's perspective, but the techniques that I share can work for anyone. It was at that very moment that I knew that it was time to write the book aimed at anyone who has a desire, who has a vision, dream, or goal that has not yet been realized. Then the words "Mind Your Vision: 2020 and Beyond" popped into my thoughts, and immediately I knew it was the book title.

This book will help you develop or improve your language of faith. You will learn how to mold your thoughts just as a potter molds clay into what he or she envisions. Our thoughts influence us to either believe or to doubt. Our thoughts can bring hope or they can cripple us with fear. *As we think, so are we.* What do you envision for your life? Is your life in focus? We have entered into the year of 2020. It's your year to gain clarity and focus. The word acuity means sharpness or keenness of thought, vision, or hearing. This book will help you sharpen your thoughts and improve your mind's-eye vision.

Since we are in the year of 2020, let's do a comparison to normal eyesight. 20/20 vision is the term used for normal visual acuity. 20/20 vision is defined as clarity or sharpness of vision measured at a distance of twenty feet. A person who has

20/20 vision can see things clearly that are twenty feet away. If you have ever had an eye exam, you were asked to read the alphabet letters displayed at the bottom of the eye exam chart. If your eyesight was clearly focused, you could easily read those letters without the need of assistance.

My goal and intent for this book is to instill within you *acuity*, to assist you in bringing clarity, focus, and faith to multiple areas of your life so that you can transform your dreams and goals into reality.

This book includes a compilation of my life experiences and techniques used that help me attain my vision, goals, and dreams. Some of the stories shared were inspired by blockbuster featured films. For the past ten years, I have inspired others through teaching the same techniques in workshops, small groups, personal coaching, conferences, and on empowerment broadcast calls. Tote-a-Vision is one of the faith tools that I reference often throughout this book.

Having your visual reminder with you is a strong reinforcement of your goals. The portability of the Tote-a-Vision simplifies the vision board-making process and provides a place for you to view your board while on the go. In the provided journal, you can track your progress, plans, ideas, affirming statements, and more.

Within my audio training program, "Manifest More of My Dreams," you will discover the methodology behind the manifestations. Anyone can create a vision board, set it, and forget it. But, if you want those things visually represented on your board to become a reality, there are key things that you need to be doing. Find out what and how to accelerate your results in "Manifest More of My Dreams" at:
www.mooreofrachel.com. I celebrate your success because you have what it takes to win.

"We must have perseverance and above all confidence in ourselves. We must believe that we are gifted for something and that this thing must be attained."

– Marie Curie, 1867-1934, physicist

Chapter 1: Find Clarity

In life, we often wear many hats of responsibility. It's so easy to become lost in all your roles that you tend to lose yourself. Your world around you needs you to be your best and do your best. That starts with you, finding clarity to mind your vision. It starts with clarifying who you are and defining what you truly want in life. As you do this, you will transform from the inside out. Then, your will have what it takes to transform your dreams and goals into reality.

I'm a working mom. I have four children. I'm a full-time engineer and an entrepreneur. If that isn't enough, I also work as an empowerment coach. I love helping others—just like you—to break through to their greatest purpose. I have a lot of responsibilities on me as the primary breadwinner here in our home. At work, I am a manager and I have several people who report to me. I sometimes find it easy to become overwhelmed and distraught by the many responsibilities I have in my life.

I can still remember the day my husband came home and told me he lost his job. It was like the weight of the world crashed down on top of me and I was the only one left to carry it. I was emotional. I felt completely helpless and stuck. I thought I had no way to change my circumstances. Here I was, the lesser of the two incomes in our house, trying to provide everything. My job had always been there so that our family could have the lifestyle that we wanted. We could go on vacations, our children could attend certain schools and have the life that I always wanted them to have. Now, it was all on me.

During our financial struggles, I found that I had to change my mindset or be crushed under the weight of the responsibility I was now carrying. I began to look for information and discovered what it means to be financially free. More importantly, I found myself asking, "What parts of my life can I control?" It's easy to want to control everything; all the aspects of our lives and all the people around us. But, the truth is, in the end, the only person we have control over is ourselves.

I know from experience that if you don't embrace this mindset and realize how to live your best life, it will impact all the areas of your life. For me, it came up as health issues. Bottled-up emotions and stress had my neck and shoulder muscles in spasms for nearly five years. I searched everywhere for the right medical help. I wanted to know why my muscles were so tight that they caused excruciating pain and discomfort almost continuously. My trapezoids were literally trapped. I began to realize that I had to let go of my focus on others and on circumstances that I couldn't change. I had to get the right mindset. I began to learn to breathe calmly and to change my perspective by refocusing my thoughts. As I directed my focus to the aspects of my life that I could control, I found that even my physical body began to feel much better.

Whatever you desire to be, do, or have in your life is *possible*. Manifesting your vision, dreams, and goals are possible! It starts with a strong desire, mental focus and clarity. When you begin to *believe to receive*, spiritual laws will be activated to operate in your favor; then situations, circumstances, and opportunities will begin to occur to position you in the path of what you are longing to receive.

It's up to you to take each step as you are led down paths of fulfillment. Don't be misguided by appearances or even the pain that you may be experiencing in your life. Some situations may not appear to be a blessing, but there are lessons to be learned. As you work through the process, things will unfold.

Focus on What You Can Change

When someone in your life lets you down, it's easy to focus only on that person. The truth of the matter is, you don't have the power to change this person. So you must focus on what you can change. You need to get your eyes off that person and focus on what you want in your life. What do you want your family to be like? What do you want your children's lives to look like? What do you want for your life? With this clarity, you will discover the steps needed to take your life and your family's life to that place.

Ask yourself, "What are the changes that I can make?" Now, focus on those. Hold them close. Knowing what you can do is the first step in finding peace of mind and happiness. The next question is to ask yourself what makes you happy. It's easy to fall into the trap of pointing fingers, assigning blame and maybe even spending all our time angry at that person in your life. Embrace tools like The Serenity Prayer; "God, grant me the serenity to accept the things I cannot change, the courage to change the things I can, and the wisdom to know the difference." You can't change people. However, you can make changes in your life and your environment. You can make changes in your mental attitude about your life. Again, it all comes down to one thing; "clarity."

Knowing what you can do is the first step in finding peace of mind and happiness.

Your mindset impacts everything in your life. That is why you must "mind your vision." You should hold dear the vision that you create for your life and be mindful of it. Then, do whatever it takes to get you there.

Finding Clarity

Where are you at this point in your life?

1. **You know what you want:** You know clearly what you want, where you want to go, what you want to do, and have in life. You are actively working towards your goals, but want additional tools and techniques to enhance your results.

2. **You know some of what you want:** You know some of your dreams, but are not really clear on what you want. You want clarity and want to discover those dreams and goals as you go through the process of reading this book and in creating a vision board.

3. **You don't know what you want, but you want to start defining what you want now:** You are at a point in life where you have stopped dreaming because of life circumstances happening to you versus you making life happen. You lost your way, and you want to find it. You want to create a dream. You want to create a new vision.

Whether you find yourself at point one, two, or three, now is a good time to envision what you want.

To envision is to imagine something to be true.

What do we use to "imagine"?

- Our MINDS
- Our imagination creates vision

We think with our minds, but we also have the ability to produce mental images in our minds. Let's stir up some creativity by using our imagination with our first exercise.

Envisioning - Exercise

You will need to go to the website link provided below to view a short video to see the images displayed. Write down words that relate to the images being shown. Next to those words, write what they mean to you.

https://mindyourvision.com/envisioning/

Did you view the video to see the images? How did you feel when you saw images that relate to your desires?

Almost everyone desires to be a homeowner. Even if you own a home at this time, it may not be your "dream home." You can envision your dream home.

Here's a one-minute exercise. Close your eyes. Now begin to imagine the house of your dreams. I want you to produce a mental image of the house that you desire. You're standing outside, maybe looking from a street view. You see the landscape, the trees, the green grass, and the architecture of your home. Now, I want you to open the door and walk inside. It's fully and beautifully decorated. Notice the open space, the high ceilings. Now take a walk through some of the rooms. See yourself looking out of the window or seated on the couch. Now open your eyes. For those of you who were able to see the images mentally, how did this visioning exercise make you feel? Did it make you feel happy? Did it wake up some excitement on the inside?

Well, that's what envisioning does. It causes you to hope for a better future. It stirs up hope!

Now, I know that some of you probably struggled with the exercise. It's sometimes hard to make your mind focus. Focus takes practice. Most of the logical, more dominant left brain thinkers may struggle because logic requires data and facts, not images unless the image is a histogram or Pie chart. The dominant right brain thinker is more creative, and producing mental images comes more naturally for them.

Sometimes the envisioning process may be hindered by other causes. You must determine what's clouding your mind's-eye vision.

What's Clouding Your Vision?

- Doubt
- Negative thinking
- Focused on current circumstances
- Can't see the forest for the trees
- People with negative attitudes
- Disobedience to Divine instructions
- Fear

Okay, here's your own set of "Vision Glasses." Put them on, mentally. We are now all wearing our vision glasses; the temperature or climate is just right and conducive for our vision to be clear. But, once we go outside into the cold temperatures, what usually happens when you are wearing eyeglasses or sunglasses? They become covered with a cloud of fog or condensation. Likewise, doubt and negativity can cloud your vision. We must neutralize the atmosphere, wiping away any negative thoughts or words that contradict our vision by counteracting with a positive response.

You must take control of your mental thermostat by blocking doubt out! Make a decision to not allow negative thoughts or negative words to cloud your vision. Neutralize the atmosphere by wiping away any negative thoughts or words that contradict your vision. Replace every negative thought with a positive one.

Refer to the Master Your Mindset chapter for techniques on how to change your internal talk track, as well as explore how to use a positive mental attitude to block out doubt.

Chapter 2: Bring Your Life In Focus

The Four Connection Quadrants

You need clarity in the four quadrants that connect you to this world. All aspects of your life fall within one of the four connection quadrants: Personal, Relationship, Financial/Work/Academic, and Community Service. You will bring your life in focus as you become clear about what you desire within each quadrant.

Personal Connection Quadrant

After letting go of what I could not control, it became clear that my physical health was closely linked to my emotional well-being. Now, I am more conscious of how my thoughts influence my emotions and behavior. Over time, I was able to develop a personal health regimen as a way to improve my stress management. It involves weekly weight training, deep breathing and relaxation techniques, visualization, and mindset management.

Your personal quadrant is all about you. It includes your spiritual life, as well as your emotional, intellectual, and physical well-being. What are you doing to become your best self? Create a goal to make your soul whole. What are your interests that you never have time for? Do you feel like you're living the life you intended? How is your emotional and physical health? How is your spiritual life? If you are not happy with where you are, do something about it.

Create a vision for your health and fitness. What is your target? Is it working through chronic pain? Do you have a weight loss or blood pressure goal? Visualize what your life could look like. Make it personal. Think about the next level. What knowledge or skills are required to reach the next level? Each person's self-improvement goals are different, but each one is important. Be specific.

Strengthen the spiritual aspect of your life. I firmly believe in divine inspiration. To create the right mindset, we must embrace the power of belief. Belief is tied closely to the mind. As you adopt your beliefs and seek spiritual insight, you will be motivated to reach your goals. The key element in minding your vision is willingness and commitment to faith in action.

In my role as an empowerment coach, I serve people by helping them break free to a new mindset that serves their purpose. I once had a client come to me with a situation he had been dealing with since his childhood—like old messages from the past. I helped him understand that once he gained control of the aspects of his life that he had control over, then he could break away from those messages of the past and move on to the bright future ahead of him.

Once you break free of unnerving thoughts from the past, you are ready to propel into your greatness. I had to break through the memories of a traumatizing experience that I had while reciting a monologue in front of my high school literature classmates. I mistook their laughter as ridicule. Then, for more than ten years, I was afraid of public speaking. I forced myself through it, but I was still afraid. I knew it was something I had to overcome, so I spent a lot of time attending Dale Carnegie and Toastmaster classes. I sought out training and gained greater understanding, which helped reshape my mindset from a place of fear to a place that allows me to speak out to help others. One of the keys to breaking through is following through.

Community Connection Quadrant
Community connection is about making a difference in the lives of people within your realm of influence. This quadrant is about your service to others. When you give of yourself in some fashion, you gain a sense of fulfillment and significance. For many years, the worship arts ministry was my community connection. I taught liturgical dance and practical steps to creating a lifestyle of worship. Married couple's ministry is another area where I love to serve. In more recent years, I have led small groups in my home, focusing on teaching others how to live their best lives. In each case, encouraging others to live their lives more abundantly provided me with life. Where does community service fit best for you during this season of your life? Opportunities to give back to your community could include volunteering at your kid's school, at a shelter, or at church.

The Community Connection Quadrant is not just about serving others, but it's also about connecting with people who can support your vision. A friend of mine, whom I met through a network marketing endeavor, invited me to a mastermind group whose primary purpose is to connect positive-minded people to a wealthy mindset. Each morning, we met via phone conference to listen to inspiring messages shared either by the call host or guest speakers. Listening to the daily teachings provided me with empowering information that nurtured my mind. That call became my "morning vitamin."

This inspiring community has served me in many ways. On one occasion, several of the group members attended an event held in Atlanta. A variety of powerful speakers graced the stage, but one woman's story pulled at my heartstrings. She started out as a single mother on government assistance, with less than $12 in her bank account. She overcame many challenges and eventually founded her company. She closed her presentation by sharing her desire to take her company public and invited the crowd to invest in her dream. That night, I bought into her dream and entered a whole new community. I continue to gain new friends from each connection.

Relationship Connection Quadrant

Often, you will find that one of these four quadrants is your primary focus. Family is a big part of the relationship quadrant. It is common for the kids to be a young mother's principal focus. Love relationships are also a big part. Whether you are single, married, or divorced, you can still desire more in a love relationship. If you are married, it's okay to envision the two of you doing more together. It's okay to desire for your love to grow stronger. If your heart longs for more or longs for an ideal love relationship, it's time to create your vision. The Tote-a-Vision can help simplify the envisioning and creative process.

During one particular workshop, a young lady was sitting with a blank stare on her face. She told me that she didn't really know what she wanted. I encouraged her to flip through the magazines until certain pictures or words began to resonate. After clipping the first picture, it was non-stop until her masterpiece was almost done. I walked up to her and said," Wow, it looks like you are creating a *love relationship* vision. She replied, "It just happened to turn out this way. I saw this dress first, then all of the other images and words just flowed." I told her that I would assist by looking for a handsome man to add to her love relationship vision. After pasting him in, her board was complete.

About six weeks later, she emails me with a praise report. She was so excited about her recent transformation. She wrote, "I literally went from zero to hero. So many men have shown up in my life and at least three are marriage potential." Then, about six months later she sends another update to let me know that she was engaged and the guy looked similar to the guy on her board. I was truly amazed!

On another instance, a more mature woman attended one of my Small Group sessions. She was divorced, but praying for a new love. During the "Create Your Tote-a-Vision" session, she found images and words to reflect exactly what she wanted to experience in her life. She is now remarried and living her dream life. Her business expanded, and she and her husband recently purchased their dream home together.

My oldest son recently decided to incorporate elements of what the woman of his dreams would entail, such as her character, mindset about life, adventure, nutrition, fitness and more on his vision board. This is his year to explore and to discover friendship that will lead to an ideal love relationship.

I shared these three different relationships to emphasize the importance of being intentional in creating a vision for your ideal relationship.

Financial Connection Quadrant

The relationship quadrant is often strongly linked to the financial quadrant. Finances determine how you perceive what you can do in the relationship quadrant. What can you provide for your children? What house do you live in? What lifestyle do you want? What vacations will you and your family take? Framing the right mindset around your finances is important. Instead of focusing on what you cannot have, focus on moving forward.

What can you do right now to enhance your relationships or your finances? When I asked myself that question, I looked around and found that I could do a little bit of sewing. For a while, I made bridesmaids dresses and window treatments for others. Sewing was not my purpose in life, but it brought in extra money. I joined several multi-level marketing companies over the years, and although they weren't my true purpose in life either, I am grateful that they led me to materials that helped me create the right mindset. I learned how to become more confident and gained a better understanding of my ability to influence my finances and success in all aspects of my life.

When you look at your finances, you know where you are. Where would you like to be? Who are the people living that kind of life that you can study? Check into the lives of millionaires, people who are working six-figure jobs, or whatever your financial goal is. Look at what they have done so you can do it, too. For me, I taped an image of a million dollars to my mirror as a reflection of prosperity and a reminder of abundance.

The financial quadrant also includes work, business, career, academic, or educational goals.

Ask yourself the question: What can you do to move toward your goal? Are there other job opportunities where you work? Is there a potential promotion on the horizon? Should you consider changing careers? Do you need to pursue specific education? Keep in mind that the only person you can control is yourself, so choose wisely and go in the direction needed to fulfill your dreams.

After you have gone through the specifics of all four quadrants, you should create a vision board that includes all your goals. I will cover this topic more in the next chapter. These visual pictures and words are great reminders as to where you want to go in life. A vision board helps to establish a goal-focused mindset.

It can include these elements of life:
- Personal growth (spiritual, emotional, mental)
- Relationships (spouse, children, family, friends)
- Health and wellness
- Work (career/business/financial/academic)
- Home/lifestyle
- Ministry and missions
- Special projects or areas of interest
- FUN, rest, and relaxation

There are opportunities that you can take advantage of right now to help make progress toward the visions that have for each area in your life. You must take specific movements in each area of your life to make progress, to improve, or to change a situation for the better. Those movements or action steps are a part of the dance of your life. The more you practice creating new good habits, the more you stretch yourself to learn new things, the more you learn to press in, versus giving up, you are becoming a better dancer. I share more about becoming a better dancer in the **Influence Your Destiny** chapter.

Get Clarity within the Quadrants:

Assignment: Write a few bullet points about where you are right now in all quadrants of your life.

(Be specific, be precise, be truthful with your answers.)

Personal Improvement - Mind, Body, and Spirit Quadrant

My Thought Life (positive or negative—are your thoughts helping or hurting your progress?)

_____
_____
_____

My Health and Fitness

_____
_____
_____

My Emotions and Spirit

_____
_____
_____

Relationships Quadrant

_____
_____
_____
_____
_____
_____
_____

Financial and Educational Quadrant

_____
_____
_____
_____
_____
_____
_____
_____

Community - Making a Difference Quadrant

_____
_____
_____
_____
_____
_____
_____
_____

Assignment: Now write what you want to experience in each quadrant. These are areas that you want to up-level and transform into a better you or into a better experience.

Up-level - to transform and grow in an area previously stagnant. For example, this year, I plan to up-level my personal brand.

Personal Improvement - Mind, Body, and Spirit Quadrant: *Personal Health and Wellness (Physical, Emotional, and Spiritual)*

Example: I want to up-level my life with my thoughts being more positive

My thought life

_____
_____
_____
_____
_____
_____

My Health and Fitness

_____
_____
_____
_____
_____

My Emotions and Spirit

_____
_____
_____
_____
_____
_____

Relationships Quadrant:

I want to be more intentional about improving or enhancing the relationships in my life. List the relationships that you want to up-level.

_____
_____
_____
_____
_____

Financial and Educational Quadrant

_____
_____
_____
_____
_____

Community - Making a Difference Quadrant

_____
_____
_____
_____
_____

Chapter 3: Apply Focus Power

FOLLOW
ONE
COURSE
UNTIL
SUCCESSFUL

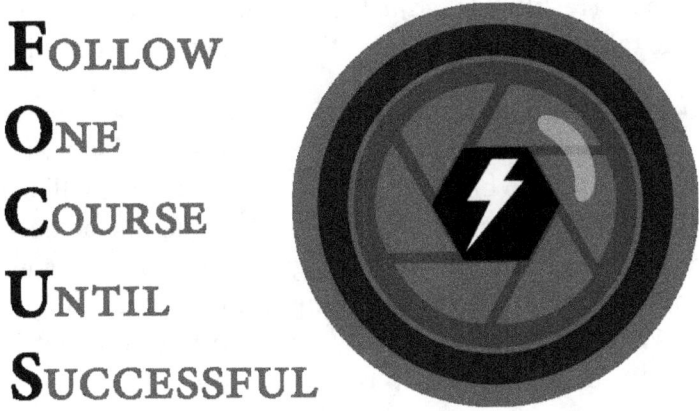

We are in a day and age where everyone has smart devices. These devices think for us and we become pretty reliant on them for a lot of things. Our smart phones connect us to the internet where we can access information at the push of a button. Our smart phones have become our shopping malls and our banks. They have become our GPS on the go and our televisions to watch the news, video, or our favorite show. We can send an instant message or we can use it as a telephone and have an audio conversation. What would we do without our phones?

Our cell phones also have cameras on them that automatically focus for us. There is no fuss with having to focus a camera lens. You just aim and take the picture. The only time we see those 35 mm Canon cameras with those big lenses attached is with an amateur photographer perfecting his skills or with a professional photographer doing a photo shoot. One of my sons loves photography and is building a business around it. He has become a student in learning the craft of photography. Whenever he works with his camera, he prefers that all of the settings be set manually. He adjusts the lens to bring the image into focus. He likes to adjust each setting, one by one, and when he takes the photographs, they come out beautifully.

When it comes to our lives, we have been given a camera. The lenses in this case are within our mind's-eye, where we must adjust for insight to bring our vision into focus. We will need to adjust different settings in our life to help us achieve the desired outcome of a beautiful image. What vision do you have for your life and what are you doing right now to bring it into focus? What are you doing right now to develop that image within your mind into your physical reality?

To help us remember the importance of focus, I've created a phrase and image to go with it. Apply FOCUS power until your goals are realized.

FOCUS

    F-Follow a course of action to completion
    O-One day at a time
    C-Course is your plan or the path
    U-Until has a definite end; when the target that you've set is achieved
    S-Successful in accomplishing the goal

Whenever you are in your life right now, it's a great time for reflection. It's time to reflect on what's happened in your life over the last six months or year.

Has life happened to you or have you made life happen over the past six to twelve months? What I mean is, have you allowed your circumstances to determine where you spend focus, effort, and time? Or have you managed your circumstances while remaining focused on achieving the goals that you set out to accomplish? If life has happened to you, it's not too late to refocus.

Have you ever wondered how some people can stay on task and fully optimize their concentration to get things done, even in the midst of distractions, delays, or disappointments? Maybe you are one of those people. But, if you are challenged on any level in remaining focused at times, this teaching will be a good one to add toward your success.

Let me give you an example of a recent time I had to adjust my focus. I received a letter regarding one of my invention patents, and it stated that they were rejecting a petition that I had made regarding a claim. My immediate thoughts were, "Okay, I give up, I'm tired, and I don't have any more energy to put toward this effort. God, I just want to give up!" So what did I do? I took a nap. I was mentally exhausted and couldn't focus on any other task, so I had to sleep it off. When I awoke, an idea popped into my head on what steps to take next.

I have to be honest, it's not easy to stay focused in the midst of disappointments, delays, and difficulties, but I have to practice what I preach. If you want to get better at controlling your thoughts, then read on! If you want to go deeper, develop your focus skills.

What to Focus:

1. Focus your thoughts and attention
2. Focus your time and energy
3. Focus your talent and effort

Where to Focus:

1. Focus on what matters
2. Focus on your goals
3. Focus on the good
4. Focus your thoughts on favorable outcomes

Where Not to Focus (or your Do Not Focus List):

1. Undesirable results
2. Negative thoughts
3. Negative circumstances
4. Negative people
5. Discouraging news

When you focus on the Do Not Focus list, these things create feelings of anxiety, fear, and worry! You could start feeling scared or discouraged when you focus your thoughts on undesirable outcomes. This was what I started to do with my patent situation, but once I had rested my mind and body, I was able to focus on the good. I gained the strength and mental fortitude to resist discouraging thoughts. We need to empower focus with happy thoughts, encouraging expectations, and optimistic outcomes.

Breaking down FOCUS

F- Follow - Follow a course of action to completion

Follow-through will help you breakthrough. Follow-through will help you break through the barrier of procrastination. Follow-through will stop the cycle of broken promises made to yourself. Follow-through will help you breakthrough to successfully completing every task that you set out to do. You want to stop falling victim to "I planned to do that or I started to do that, but never finished" syndrome.

O - *One day at a time*

Have one goal at a time for each category in your life. Plan for tomorrow (the future), but focus on today. To avoid becoming overwhelmed, focus on one day at a time. Yes, plan ahead, but focus on today and on what needs to get done today or on what needs to happen today.

Oneness is Synergy. Syn-Energy – Syn: united; acting or considered together; Energy: strength or power efficiently exerted, capacity for vigorous action, the capacity for activity or the exertion of power. When you synergize your thoughts, your will to do, and your emotions on completing a certain task, your physical body will follow through with the course actions to complete that task.

Oneness in your soul – Aligning your thoughts, will, and emotions strengthen your ability to focus.

Oneness with Divine Source – The closeness provides energy to strengthen your focus. That relationship will serve as strength and encouragement. Even when you are struggling with having positive thoughts about your situation or you don't feel like tackling a task, you can pull from the Divine Source Energy through prayer, to help pull you together. Personally, I will quote Scriptures to remind myself of God's promises and to help to refocus my thoughts, will, and emotions.

C - *Course - A course carried out brings completion*

Choose your course, choose your plan, or choose your path. Then stick to the plan until it brings your desired success or until new insight or instructions are given to improve or alter the plan for better or faster results.

Any time you take an academic course, what should you expect while you are taking that course? You should expect pop quizzes, test, or exams, right? You also expect for your knowledge to grow in whatever course you are taking at that time. You learn about that subject. Well, likewise, whenever you choose to take a course of actions, test or challenges will be set in your path and you will also be stretched to learn new information or to learn new ways of doing things.

For example, I decided to take a course of actions to explore the possibilities of owning real estate investments. I own my home, but I had to become a student and began to learn the basics of owning investment property. So, I took a few short classes and partnered with a realtor and broker who knows the trade. We started looking at properties. I had to set aside time to review each one closely and to decide what would be my next course of actions.

Then, that's when the pop quizzes started. I had to answer all of these questions, such as how much money do you want to spend on an investment property, what's your price range, what size repairs will you be able to manage, and so forth. The big test came when I started making offers on properties that I wanted to purchase and things kept falling through. All of this activity was requiring a lot of my time and energy, which reduced the amount of time that I had to focus on top priorities in the other categories of my life.

If we are completely honest, no one really likes to take tests or enjoys being faced with a huge challenge. At least I don't personally care for them, but I can't avoid them. So we have to learn how to take them and to pass them. In order to pass the test in the midst of carrying out your course, you must first recognize that the challenge is a test. Challenges or test can come in various forms:

- Unexpected expenses like a big automobile repair expense
- Unpleasant news

- Unexpected delays
- Unexpected events

Anything outside of an unexpected blessing is probably a test. But try not to lose sight of your initial purpose of starting down that path. Refocus and continue taking that course of actions until completion.

U - Until is a definite end of one thing and the beginning of something else.

Until is the line that you draw in the sand pointing toward the target that you want to achieve. Until is that time period up to that moment of success, and up to that moment of victory

For example, you might follow a certain course of actions in exercise until you lose 25 pounds. Or you follow a certain course of actions in a business plan until you increase your customer base by 50%.

S - *Successful in accomplishing the goal, the task, or the planned course of actions*

This one is pretty clear. You will know when you hit your goal!

Foundation of Focus

Decision – Make a decision. Ask yourself, "Am I going to focus and get this done or not?" Tony Robbins says, "It is in your moments of decision that your destiny is shaped." I'll add to that. *"Shape your decisions around the destiny you want to create." – Rachel Moore*

Intention and Attention – Set your intention to pay attention. Determine in your mind and your will that you will direct all of your physical energy, mental energy and emotional energy on certain tasks.

Prioritization – Choose what's important and do it first, or choose what can be done quickly and get it done.

Attitude – Your attitude will determine your response and recovery time from the unexpected. Having the right attitude will help you look past those roadblocks and delays to keep the image of that beautiful outcome in focus.

Now that you know the importance of focus and some of the keys, another thing you can do to help yourself, to help your family, or to help your team is to call a focus meeting.

1. **Personal Focus Meeting**
   Ask the following questions:

   - What are my top priorities right now?
   - What do I want to accomplish in those top priorities?
   - What task or action steps can I take to accomplish the top priorities?

Note: It's okay to have top priorities in multiple categories, like in finances, health, family, and home, but if you have multiple top priorities in the same category, then you need to prioritize that top priority list and choose one to focus on first in that category until completion.

2. **Family Focus Meeting**
   Helps to bring oneness in hearts and minds, when you discuss the areas that each of you will be focusing on over the next few months. This is something that I did with my family. I called it a "Summer Family Focus" meeting. I divided our discussion into four categories:

   - House focus
   - Academic focus
   - Building skills focus
   - Summer vacation and fun focus

House Focus
Kitchen Duty: We discussed duties for each person. Since my oldest son was going away to college in the fall, I added my youngest son to the kitchen duty list. He would wash dishes on Sundays with me so that I can train him, and the other three sons would choose their two days of the week to wash dishes and clean the kitchen.

Closet Duty: Remove all unwanted clothes, bag and label them.

Academic Focus:
Two of my sons were seniors in high school this fall. They are twins. They will be looking for colleges to attend and scheduling college tours. They will also be searching and applying for scholarships.

Building Skills Focus:
Each of my sons talked about the skills they will build over the summer (I talk about mine as well). One took a film class online, one worked on 3D modeling and painting skills, and so forth.

3. Business Focus Meeting
If you have a business team, call a meeting to review your goals or to create a specific focus for the next quarter.

Okay, let's now turn the dial to focus on writing your personal or family vision.

CHAPTER 4: WRITE THE VISION

Are you the visionary for your family? If not, you can be. Being a visionary starts with a desire to be, to do, and to have more for you and your family.

A Decade of Family Visioning

Over the past decade, my family and I have created a Family Vision Board to reflect our family goals each year. The creative process usually takes at least a half day, so we named our vision board day "Family Visioning Day." It's a time where we think about the things that we want to happen in our life individually and collectively as a family for the year. Then we write down our thoughts in bullet form on paper.

Writing your vision is an important step in finding clarity and in defining what you want. What's important to you? What do you want for yourself and for your family?

Our Family's First Experience with Vision Boards

One day in 2009, it was time to prepare for our next monthly family activity. I wanted something different. My desire was to teach our children a creative method to goal setting. While driving to work, the perfect idea came to mind. Later that evening, I gathered the required materials and added some finishing touches to my family surprise. Then the fun was ready to begin.

When the kids and my husband walked into our meeting spot at home, they were greeted with a room full of colorful magazines, scissors, glue, and my little surprise. Being the activity leader that night, I asked the questions and they had to respond in both spoken and written words. Sample of the questions were, "What would you like to do as a family over the next twelve months? "What would you like to have in your possession?" "Where would you like to go?" "What do you dream of becoming when you grow up?" I even asked them questions regarding their schoolwork and extracurricular activities.

The questions stirred up excitement. The kids were blurting out their wishes, so I encouraged them to write down their answers. Of course, I did the writing for our 4-year-old. Once all hearts were clear, we transitioned to the highlight of the evening. Everyone, including the 4-year-old, was sent on a scavenger hunt. We each had to search for and cut out pictures, images, and words that reflected our wishes. Then we filled up our individual white card stock boards and family board with the cutouts. The boys were so engaged in cutting and pasting that they were wide awake until 2 a.m. The pictures awoke hope and a belief that somehow our dreams and goals would come to fruition. The activity concluded with me giving everyone the "little surprise," a Tote-a-Vision to protect and display their new visual treasure. That night everyone went to bed with happy thoughts. Our hearts were filled with new possibilities.

We now had our individual goals and desires for our family in visual form. Our new visual treasures helped us to stay focused on our goals as we referred to them throughout the year. Some were educational goals and some were just for pure fun.

Dream with Your Kids

A few days following that family activity, I presented my four sons with a challenge. I challenged them to use their skills to create cash, and I promised that I would match whatever dollar amount they earned over the next two weeks. After making a list of all of their skills, their little heads began to spin with ideas. Well, lo and behold, in one week following our family visioning night and my "Mommy promise," an opportunity was presented for my sons to use their film production skills. They were paid to be the video production crew for a public event.

At the ages of 13, 10, 10, and 4, the boys—Jonathan, Jamicah, Jeremy, and Joshua—became the video production crew for a small local event. They did quite well with their video sales, and as a mom of her word, I kept my matching promise. They were excited about the money that they had earned.

Unbeknownst to me, it was already earmarked for something on their wish list. They made their purchase. After the unboxing of their *Guitar Hero* complete band game for Wii, Jeremy came running to me, pointing at his visual treasure.

"Mommy, Mommy, look we got it. It was on my board! See the picture? We got exactly what we wanted and it happened really fast!"

Believe me, I too was amazed at how quickly things had happened. That experience boosted our faith to believe in our hopes and dreams, no matter how big or small.

The boys had a desire to own the *Guitar Hero* band instruments and game for their Wii system.

- The boys applied faith to receive their desire.
- They placed the image on their Tote-a-Vision board.
- They believed that somehow they would receive it that year.
- They didn't doubt.
- They took my challenge and action when the opportunity presented itself to work and earn money.
- They purchased their *Guitar Hero* band game

https://mindyourvision.com/guitar-hero/

Our family's first vision board

My sons learned the importance of establishing clear goals in both written and visual form. They also learned the power of thinking positive about whatever you want in life and your dreams, goals, and wishes can come true. We learned the importance of dream building and goal setting as a family.

The boy's guitar dream come true

That one activity, which we now call "family visioning", has now become a family tradition. We had a blast working on and toward our goals the first year as a family, and we continue to get incredible results and would encourage other families to do the same with their children. Set clear goals, have faith, work hard, collaborate as a family, then watch the magic happen!

The Magic of Believing as a Family

We created our next family vision board on January 2, 2010. That day set the foundation for our annual family visioning moments. Together as a family, I had my four sons help me create our "Family Focus 2010" Tote-a-Vision board. At that time they were ages 13, 10, 10, and 4. Our major focus as a family in 2010 was family vacations and doing monthly activities as a family. That vision board represented all of the fun activities we would do together in that year, which actually helped us to put our family goals into visual form. We were able to stay focused on our goals because we referred back to the board throughout the year. Some were educational goals and some were just for pure fun.

Our plan was to have at least one family activity a month. I had the boys call out activities they wanted to do as a family in 2010. My oldest son was responsible for writing the activities down in a list format. My kids' dreams for the year were to do a lot of FUN STUFF, like laser tag, bowling, picnicking, biking, touring downtown Atlanta, and going to Disney and to the beach. Their last assignment was to search for pictures and images that represented the activities they had on the list. After finding and cutting out the images, my task was to lay them out and paste them on the Tote-a-Vision white board.

One of the educational images on the vision board was the Tech Fair robot. The three of my sons who were old enough to participate in the Bibb County Technology Fair were working on their digital animations projects, and their goal was to all win at the Tech Fair. Another image placed on the board was of Mickey Mouse at the Disneyland castle, which represented at least one of them winning first place in the International Student Media Festival that was scheduled to occur in California.

After establishing clear goals as a family, here's what happened that year. All three of my sons' projects won in the Bibb County Tech Fair. Jamicah won first place. Jonathan won second place, and Jeremy won third. We were all very excited about the results. Now they all had a chance for their projects to win at the international level.

The other educational activity shown on our board was the Phoenix International Christian Film Festival. Since my three oldest sons were into competing in technology fairs and film festivals, my dream was expose them to the Christian filmmaking industry. I knew it would cost lots of cash for our family of six to fly out to Arizona, and I also knew that the money was not in our budget. We were living on my salary since my husband was still looking for work. His answer was, "No, we can't go," but my heart did not accept no as our final answer. I knew that all things are possible to the one who believes.

My heart was set, so we placed it as a goal on our family vision board. To prepare for the festival, my family submitted three different films: a short film, a film trailer, and a product ad.

We were notified that Jamicah received a nomination for Best Youth Producer for his short film, *Honesty,* and that my Tote-a-Vision product advertisement was selected to view on the big screen during the film screening sessions. In addition, I was invited to set up a product table on the day scheduled for our film debuts. All of the excitement and anticipation made us really look forward to the festival. The airplane image on our board represented the boys' very first major airplane ride. I had them imagine being on the airplane flying to Arizona.

Our trip to Arizona was more than what we expected. Amazingly, the money came from the most unexpected source. After attending a financial wellness class at our church, I gained a better understanding of the different types of life insurance. I used that new knowledge to acquire a new policy and cashed in my old one, which provided more than enough for our family vacation. We stayed in a five-star resort and had money left over after our trip to invest into savings. A large portion of our board was focused on giving praise to God. We gave thanks and praise to Him throughout the year for His awesome provision.

While packing for our trip, I decided to fill an entire piece of luggage with Tote-a-Visions (the portable vision boards with journals). My heart's desire was to sell all of them at the Film Festival. A literal miracle happened to make my dream come true, but before I share the details, there is an interesting twist to this vacation story that started when we arrived at the airport. Our faith was tested! We almost didn't make our flight together because the time was too close to flight departure to check one piece of luggage. At first, we started to panic, but I had to remind everyone to repeat the visual exercises we practiced. I spoke a quick prayer while standing in line. Then, the attendant asked my husband to stay with the luggage and take another flight but sent the boys and me off to catch our scheduled flight before it departed.

When we arrived at the gate, people were standing around. What was really strange was that the departure time showing on the marquee had changed. I asked the attendant at the desk if we were in the right place. She assured me that it was our flight departure gate. Then she told me that they had just received a notice that the entire flight crew was running late, so the departure time had been extended.

I looked up and there was my husband. They had checked the bag and sent him on to join us. The boys and I literally jumped up and down with joy and amazement. My prayer had been answered, and our vision of us sitting on the airplane together came true. We were all blown away by such a powerful experience. We boarded the plane and filled up an entire row, just as we had planned and envisioned—three on each side of the aisle.

During our seven-day vacation, five days were filled with knowledge-packed classes at the Festival. The boys stayed intrigued the entire trip. We took classes on script writing, video editing, digital music production, improve-acting, show production, show hosting, marketing, and so much more.

While there, I attended the "How to Accomplish Your Media Dream" session. The Festival host shared several key points about goal setting from her book *Dream Big*. At the end of the session, I walked up and waited my turn to speak with the host. I went prepared. I showed her our "Family Focus 2010" vision board. I told her that attending the Media Festival was a goal that we set as a family that year. I pointed to the image of the Festival Brochure display on our board. Becoming intrigued by my story, she continued to listen. I told her how much I enjoyed her session, then handed her a Tote-a-Vision as a gift to keep. Before I walked away, she gifted me with one of her "Good Life" books and instructed me to meet her assistant at their book table to pick up the book.

This is where things get interesting. I had the opportunity to show the assistant several examples of our individual Tote-a-Vision boards. She was so impressed that she handed me a check to get one for herself. During our conversation, I shared that I had been praying for guidance on how to sell the luggage full of Tote-a-Visions that I brought with me. The assistant then proceeded to tell me that she would check with their production manager to see if they would carry my product within their bookstore. She told me that she couldn't make any promises because they were in the middle of a conference, but she would give me a call on that Friday.

Well, Friday came. It was the day of my film debut. Jamicah's *Honesty* film debut occurred earlier that week. Just outside of the screening room, I sat up a small table to display my Tote-a-Visions. Since there were other vendors around, my five-year-old son, Joshua, decided to visit other tables. He discovered a way to make money selling products that he got for free. I didn't know this until he came to me with two pockets filled with dollar bills. A gentleman at one of the tables was giving him Slinkees. Then, Joshua found people who would buy a Slinkee from him for $1. He was an entrepreneur in the making.

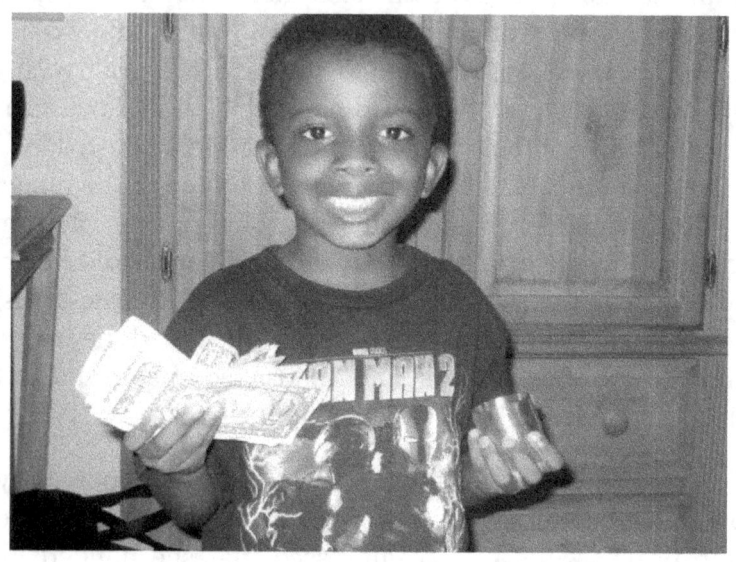

Joshua, showing off his cash

The time finally came for me to go inside to watch my product advertisement on the big screen. It was 60 seconds of bliss. Since, the *Tote-a-Vision* ad played quickly, we decided to sit through to watch some other films. My phone began to buzz, so I ran out of the room to answer the call. It was the Festival host's assistant. She called to tell me that the production manager loved my Tote-a-Vision product and wanted to know how many I brought with me. I told her around 30. She then exclaimed, "We'll take 30!" That was my miracle moment! We negotiated on a wholesale price over the phone. She asked if I could prepare an invoice to give her on Saturday so we could close the deal, and of course I said *YES*. Believe me, my heart leaped with joy, and I was so excited! My prayers were answered, and my vision to sell a luggage full of Tote-a-Visions during our trip manifested in living colors. Later that evening, we all dressed up for the Awards Ceremony. Jamicah's *Honesty* film was nominated as the *Audience Favorite*. *My sons had their first* Red Carpet experience. *See more photos from that trip at* https://mooreofrachel.com/inspire/inspire-my-family/

Four sons on the Red Carpet at the Award's Ceremony

While in Arizona, we also had the opportunity to visit one of the Seven Natural Wonders of the World, the Grand Canyon. It was massive and so beautiful. Together as a family we walked the trail that displayed the different types of rocks and the age of each layer within the canyon. We also had a family picnic during our stay at the resort. Right in front of our condo was a picnic table, grill, and cabana. The family picnic was another image that we had on our family vision board. How cool is that!

From that point on, we were hooked on the concept of visualizing and believing for a desired outcome. Out of all the family activities that we've shared together, the Tote-a-Vision experience was one that started a new family tradition and was the beginning of a new way of thinking and doing life forever.

To help close out the year with a big bang, we were notified that Jonathan's tech fair digital animation project had won first place in the International Student Media Festival. Rutland Middle School, along with family and friends, made financial contributions toward Jonathan's trip to Anaheim, California, in October. The festival planned a special educational student behind the scenes animation series for the students at Disneyland. I had the privilege to take the trip with Jonathan to California. I was very thankful for the one-on-one time with my oldest son.

In November of that same year, we reflected on our family goals shown on the Tote-a-Vision board—more than 98 percent of the activities had taken place. We had a blast working on and toward our goals as a family, and the hard work, focus, and collaboration really paid off! We continue to get similar results each year for our individual and family goals.

Visioning or dream building with Tote-a-Vision is an activity that can be adopted by other families or even schools to assist the students in setting and reaching academic, life, or extracurricular goals. For more information about Tote-a-Vision products, visit www.mindyourvision.com.

Our Family Focus Vision Board in 2010

The one thing that I will emphasize is to capture the moments as your vision or dream unfolds and comes to pass with dates, notes, and more. Within my Tote-a-Vision Journal for 2010, I captured all of the milestones and the things that happened in our 2010 Family Vision. Amazingly, almost everything that we had on our Vision Board happened that year, and I have pictures, journal notes, and even handwritten notes from my oldest son (who was 13 at that time) listing each activity that he and his brothers wanted to experience in 2010. I also attached airline tickets, movie tickets, and more within my Tote-a-Vision Journal to show how our year unfolded and captured how our dreams came true that year.

A Decade Later

Our Family Connection Focus Vision Board in 2020

On January 4, 2020, before starting our Family and Friends Visioning Day this year, we reflected on each of our vision boards that we created over the past ten years. It was neat having my journal to show them the details of what took place. My youngest son especially benefited from flipping through my journal because he was too young to remember what happened at 4 years old.

Within this digital age, we capture moments on our smart phones and smart devices, but often fail to write down those milestones or even collect mementos along the way. Since it's so easy to lose digital photos and videos, I challenge you to put more concrete methods in place this year to record or capture your special life events.

Now that three of my sons are in college, our family focus is finding meaningful ways to connect. Our 2020 Family Vision Board reflects all the ways we desire to connect this year.

Praying together is placed in the center of our board because prayer is a connection that makes a stronger family. We connect over phone conversations and group FaceTime calls. "Let There Be Light" is our desire for God's presence and guidance to be with us as we live, work, and play. We will also connect as we celebrate each other's outstanding achievements throughout the year. We look forward to connecting this year through family adventures, family road trips, movie nights, art exhibits, music, and dining out—all to *Make Moore HAPPY Memories!*

What is your family 2020 vision and beyond? Take time to have a family discussion about your desires as a family and as individuals. So, what is your dream? As Dr. Martin Luther King said when he shared his dream, "I've been to the mountaintop." Have you been to the mountaintop?

The mountaintop represents seeing all of the possibilities that could happen in your life by going to the heights in your imagination. To dream, and to dream BIG! To not allowing circumstances or situations to cause you not to dream, but to work toward those dreams and to take action daily, to have faith, hope, and resilience to move forth in the things that you desire. Dr. King lived for greatness, and we too can live for greatness and do those things that we desire to achieve. We can all have a dream. What is your dream today? What do you want to manifest in your life?

The Visioning Process

The visioning process incorporates both the written and visual aspects of vision

A *vision* is futuristic and has not yet happened. A vision of what you desire should be written down. Mental images and thoughts can create visions of things desired. Hence, a vision board tells a visual story of where a person desires to go, wants to achieve, or hopes to attain.

Our mind and imagination control our free will. What you believe way down deep inside will determine your results. If you believe and doubt not, you can have what you say. Faith is believing that those things that you're hoping for will be.

What did Jesus say to the woman with the issue of blood? "Daughter...thy faith hath made thee whole" (Matthew 9:22 KJV). She saw herself healed. She knew that if she could just touch the hem of His garment, that she would be healed. She pressed her way through the crowd, even in her pain and weakness.

Like the lady who pressed her way through the crowd to be healed, some of us can press our way toward our vision without the aid of any help or tool; while on the other hand, some of us need something to help boost our faith to believe for the vision. We need pictures. Faith needs a picture.

Vision Board/Dream Board – Puts a Picture on Your Faith

A vision board or dream board simply displays images or words representing things and experiences you desire in your life. There are different forms of vision boards you can create. General vision boards are common when you want to capture desires you have for multiple areas of your life. Themes work well when you want to showcase details regarding a specific area of your life, such as your business, home, health, or a relationship.

The traditional vision boards on large poster boards are usually placed somewhere in your home or office to reference as needed, but they are usually too big to carry with you. Goals are easier to achieve when you can continually focus on them.

What is Family Visioning?

Family visioning is NOT just about writing a family vision or mission statement.

Let's first define "family vision."

A family vision is based on your values, and it states how you will conduct your lives. We created our family vision several years ago. As a mom, I took it a step further to create a "Mommy Mission" vision, where I defined my commitment to be a role model for my sons and described the things that I desired to see manifest in my sons' lives.

Assignment: Write a personal or family vision statement / mission statement that includes your values and how you want to conduct your lives as a family.

_____
_____
_____
_____
_____
_____
_____
_____
_____
_____
_____
_____
_____

A family vision is a good start, but Family Visioning is different in the sense that you discuss desires, goals, hopes and dreams. Family Visioning consist of writing those things down. Then, you take it a step further and find images that reflect those things.

Family visioning is a time when the family:

- Sits down to discuss and write down the family's desires, goals, hopes, and dreams
- Finds images and power words that represent those things
- Each person should create their own Tote-a-Vision board first. Then everyone can collectively provide input toward the creation of a Family Tote-a-Vision board.
- Pastes them onto white Tote-a-Vision board
- Each person should show off their new inspirational work of art and share the meaning of the images or words within their vision

Benefits of Family Visioning

- Experience the power of agreement
- Puts everyone on the same page in plans for the year
- It gives everyone a sense of direction
- Promotes unity—united in mind or purpose
- It fosters collaboration (working together with others to achieve a common goal), cooperation, and agreement
- Stirs up creativity

Assignment: Write in a journal or notebook

Write the vision—write down what you desire to see fulfilled in your life, in all areas of your life:

Mind Your Vision: 2020 and Beyond

- Spiritual, relationships, health, business, finances, etc.
- Then give your vision a picture to solidify and strengthen your faith (a picture is worth a thousand words)
- Your faith needs a picture. Pictures help to increase belief, minimize doubt, and diminish discouraging thoughts.

What is Tote-a-Vision?

- Tote-a-Vision—a faith-building tool. Use it to create a portable size vision board.
- We need the proper tools to help get a job done faster and more proficiently
- Tote-a-Vision is not magic; it's a goal-setting tool that you can use to keep your desires and goals before you at all times
- It's a tool to help keep you focused on where you're going
- It exercises your faith. You have to believe that what you desire is true
- Track your progress. A journal is provided with Tote-a-Vision

Are you ready to be creative? Within the next chapter you can prepare to create.

Scriptures about Vision

Habakkuk 2:23: "And the Lord answered me, and said, 'Write the vision, and make it plain upon tables, that he may run that readeth it.

For the vision is yet for an appointed time, but at the end it shall speak, and not lie: though it tarry, wait for it; because it will surely come, it will not tarry.'"

Proverbs 29:18: "Where there is no vision, the people perish: but he that keepeth the law, happy is he."

Chapter 5: Prepare To Create

We all have dreams in our heart that we want to come true, right? In this chapter, you will write down some of the things that you want and create your vision board. We are hoping for something to happen in our lives. We are hoping that our desires form into tangible substance that we can see, feel, and experience.

We will need to focus on the things that will help us to accomplish those dreams. The substance of things hoped for... "Now faith is the substance of things hoped for, the evidence of things not seen." Hebrews 11:1, King James Version (KJV)

(I'll discuss faith in more detail later.)

Process – Progress - Success

1. Define your vision, desires, goals and dreams (write them down). Use your Tote-a-Vision. Keep all of your dreams, vision and goals in one place.
2. Create Visual Representation (Vision Board / Dream Board / Tote-a-Vision).
3. Mindset shift
4. Me Daily Habits
5. Define Dream / Vision Plan
6. Action (Productive Activity)
7. Results – Results - Results

75% - Seventy-five percent of whatever we're trying to accomplish is based on three things:

- Thoughts (25 percent)
- Words (25 percent)
- Feelings (25 percent)

These three things all formulate from the mind. Action is the other 25 percent remaining and is required to getting results.

All four of these things must be congruent and in alignment. If any of these don't line up, then you won't get the results that you want.

You can start to get your thoughts, words, and feelings into alignment and decide on your action steps by answering these questions here or in a separate journal.

What is it I want right now that will improve my life? Is it...

- Great health and fitness
- Happy connected family
- Abundant cash flow
- Financial freedom/wealth
- Dream relationship
- Dream home
- Dream job or career
- New business venture with greater cash flow potential
- Get out of debt and into financial freedom
- Make a difference in the lives of others
- Other:

_____
_____
_____
_____
_____

Ask yourself these questions:
- What do I want?
- What do I want to do?
- What do I want to become?
- What do I want to learn?
- What do I want to have or obtain?
- What do I want to give in return?
- Am I making the best use of my time on a daily basis?
- Do my thoughts and actions align with where I desire to go in life?

My Personal Goals as I Know them right now:

Write IT

Write the vision—Write down what you desire to see fulfilled in your life, in all areas of your life: spiritual, relationships, health, business, finances, etc. Next, you'll give your vision a picture to solidify and strengthen your faith.

Date_____

_____
_____
_____
_____
_____
_____
_____
_____
_____
_____
_____
_____
_____
_____

Picture IT

It's time to have a party! Have a Tote-a-Vision board party to make this a fun event. Gather with family or with some friends to create your vision boards together.

Faith needs a picture. Putting a picture on your faith helps to increase belief and minimize doubt.

If you choose **not** to have a group event, choose at least one other person to share your goals with. Having another person involved is an essential piece to holding you accountable to following through on your goals. The lack of accountability is the reason many people don't finish what they start.

Now it's time for the fun part. Search for images, pictures, word art, and power words that reflect and represent the desires that you wrote down.

Lay out several different types of magazines around you, such as business or money, travel, home and garden, and family magazines. Or do an online search and print out images you want to use.

Cut and paste the items onto the white board provided with the Tote-a-Vision workbook. Fill in as much white space as possible with your images and power words.

Your completed Tote-a-Vision board will become your daily inspiration. Visit www.mooreofrachel.com for examples of Tote-a-Vision boards created in a variety of themes.

Tote IT

Insert your completed vision board into the large clear vinyl pocket of the Tote-a-Vision sleeve.

Place a composition notebook inside the sleeve of the Tote-a-Vision. Now you're ready to tote your vision everywhere you go to keep you focused on your goals. Or you may choose to display it flat.

Before you proceed, complete (or at least start) your Tote-a-Vision board. It's a very important step.

Your Tote-a-Vision board is complete. Now what?

Get IT to Flow

Start to experience everyday miracles as you witness your vision, dreams, and goals become reality. To accelerate your results, learn the methodology behind the manifestation in the Manifest More of My Dreams audio training program at https://mooreofrachel.com/manifest-more-program/

The Top 10 Reasons Tote-a-Vision Will Change Your Life

A vision is a terrible thing to waste. Everybody has his or her own visions and goals in life. However, not everybody is courageous enough to face life's challenges. Here are the top ten reasons Tote-a-Vision can change your life and help you move forward.

1. Your Objectives Are Outlined: By defining your goals and aspirations, you are setting directions of how you will move on with life. Just like a captain of a ship, you expect to get to your destination, and you will be ready for the rewards at the end of the journey. You now begin laying out plans on how to effectively reach your dreams. Thus, you are giving more meaning to your life.
2. You Will Become Motivated: Inspiration is one of your greatest motivators. Through the use of Tote-a-Vision, you will become more inspired in pushing the edge so you can achieve your hopes and dreams. By being constantly reminded of your wishes, you will move toward achieving your goals.

3. **You Will Become Less Distracted:** By training your mind to maintain its focus, you will pay less attention to many distractions. You will learn how to eliminate your anxieties and fears. Just like an archer, you will pay less attention to what others are saying and only having in mind targeting that bull's eye.
4. **You Will Believe More in Yourself:** When your goals are clearly outlined by you, challenging yourself to make them happen will transpire naturally. You will become enthusiastic in tracking your progress and milestones as well as realizing that you can do it. Thus, you will attract many positive things along the way.
5. **You Will Be Able to Balance Circumstances:** The desire of meeting your goal is a given fact. However, the means of getting there may not be as easy as it sounds. Tote-a-Vision will help you analyze the most efficient and effective ways of achieving your goals. You will be able to weigh the pros and cons of a certain action.
6. **You Will Learn and Understand More:** As you walk toward your goal, there will be times where some of your actions deliver unexpected results. Failure to hit a particular mark should be positively viewed since it will open new doors for learning. When you learn through experience, you understand. Therefore, you will be more thoughtful of your next activities. Thus, you will have a positive attitude toward executing your next strategy.
7. **You Will Become Positive to Welcome Change:** Changes may not be appealing every time because there are situations that may not be moving according to your plan. However, the burning passion of meeting your goals will help you look into the hidden significance of such changes. You will positively seek opportunity in times of adversity.
8. **You Will Attract Positive-Minded Friends:** Friends are important contributors in life. However, in meeting your goals, it is crucial to encircle your life with positive-minded

friends. You will be surprised that Tote-a-Vision will help you attract these types of people who will help you make your dreams come true. They will give you encouragements and inspirations that could help you become victorious in your own battle.

9. You Will Inspire Others: Even without you knowing, you are gradually inspiring people around you by showing a positive attitude on things you do. However, when you are aware that you are indeed empowering others so they could also achieve their goals, it could give you much gladness, which makes you move forward so to further inspire them.
10. You Will Become Happy: This is the most important gift that your Tote-a-Vision could give to you. The happiness brought by completing your quests is undeniably priceless.

In addition, Tote-a-Vision is handy, and you can carry it with you anytime and anywhere. This will best assist you in battling out negativities as well as thoughts of lack along the way. You will no longer misplace your mission statement or list of goals. You will no longer forget the affirmations and the power Scriptures because they will always be with you every time.

Should you wake up every morning feeling uncertain of what to do, your Tote-a-Vision will help you refocus. Tote-a-Vision can help you redefine your life for the better.

Chapter 6: Master Your Mindset

FAITH ZONE

YOUR VISION DREAMS & DESIRES — New Mindset — COMFORT ZONE — New Habits — YOUR PURPOSE & DESTINY

Get out of your comfort zone and into the Faith Zone. Get comfortable with being uncomfortable. Let's be real, it's uncomfortable to walk by faith and not by sight. It's uncomfortable to believe for what seems impossible. It's uncomfortable to believe for the possibilities of your vision, dreams, and desires actually manifesting into reality. When you live in the Faith Zone, you are developing a new mindset and new habits, all of which are necessary to reach your highest dreams, purpose, and destiny.

No Longer Resist the Possibilities

It starts with a feeling on the inside of you that there is more to life for you than the present. If you embrace the thought, then God will start to grow that desire in you. You can embrace the next larger part of yourself. It's new potential and new possibilities being discovered.

Changing our old mindset and transforming your mind and your daily habits are key to transforming the desires, dreams, and goals you just put on your vision board into reality. The next step is the process of creating new daily habits that will keep you in the right state, in a positive state of mind and an emotional state of feeling good about all aspects of your life.

Usually, experiences build a reference point in your mind. Then the next thing that comes along that looks similar or reminds you of the last experience—whether it be good or bad—you will make that your reference point before making a decision. And if there is no reference point, you will sometimes allow fear to come in and rob you of the next possibility.

Mindset Matters

You may have been asking, how do you mind your vision? "Mind your vision" has a three-part meaning that will be revealed over the next several pages.

First, to mind your vision, you must instill the right information in your mind to create the necessary thoughts to reach your goals. A fortified mindset allows you to have a healthy perspective on your current situation and about your future.

If you want to experience different results in an area of your life, you must first change your thought pattern. Your most dominant thoughts will drive your life. When you change your thought track, you literally transform your mind, which in turn transforms the results in your life.

Let us take a quick inventory of the thoughts you processed today. Ask yourself the following questions:

- What have I been thinking about over the last hour? What about the last twenty-four hours?
- Did I feel anxious, discouraged, afraid, or doubtful?

If you answered "yes" to the second question, you probably had thoughts that were negative or they contradicted what you want to experience. For example, when my family thought we would miss our flight for our vacation, we started to feel panic and fear. But when I reminded everyone to keep visualizing us being on the airplane together, we stayed calm and hopeful. As a result, what we wanted came true. We had to maintain a state of belief in our minds. If your answer was "no" and you had neutral or positive feelings, then your thoughts were probably in alignment with your desires.

Our feelings are like temperature sensors; they can detect hot or cold stimulants. Positive thoughts produce warm emotions, while negative thoughts create cold moods. Our thoughts are the stimulants to our emotional system. Our feelings are a good indication of the type of thoughts we are processing. Positive and negative thoughts bring about different emotions, such as happy or sad, calm or anxious, and grateful or resentful.

Thoughts trigger feelings, and feelings trigger responses. To "feel good" or to be in a peaceful state, we must monitor our thoughts and keep them in alignment with our desired outcomes. Our eyes and ears are gates to our soul. What we see through our eyes and hear with our ears can influence our thoughts and feelings. So it is important for us to guard the gates to our soul. Input only what is beneficial and productive to maintaining a healthy mindset. Our most dominant thoughts influence our actions.

Take control of your mental thermostat and block doubt out! Thoughts and words that are negative produce doubt. Focusing your thoughts on past negative experiences can induce doubt. Negative words from others can trigger doubtful thoughts too.

The first step to removing negativity is to filter out the negative influences. Neutralize the atmosphere of your mind by eliminating thoughts or words that contradict your life vision. Neutralization occurs as you counteract negative thoughts or words with a positive response or positive thought. Superimpose positive thoughts over the negative thoughts. This must become a common practice so that the positive outweighs the negative.

Say aloud, "I choose to avoid negative thoughts or negative words that produce doubt in my mind."

"I chose to dominate the negative with the positive."

Here a few "mindful methods" to renew your mindset:

- Monitor your mindset to identify self-sabotaging thought patterns.
- Substitute negative thoughts with empowering thoughts. Ask yourself, "Is this what I want or is it fear?" Replace thoughts that contradict your desires with thoughts that align with your goals.
- Recondition your mind by inputting positive information from books or inspirational messages. Expand your knowledge and gain understanding.
- Create a list of reaffirming statements to confirm what you want out of life. Read and recite statements such as, "I am a winner" and "I have greatness in me."
- Cultivate creativity by thinking about what you want to manifest in your life. Visualize the desired outcome.
- Create a visual reminder such as the Tote-a-Vision to help stay focused on what you want.

- Meditate on Scripture, inspirational quotes, positive literature, or podcasts to condition your attitude.

Filling your mind with quality information will motivate you and condition your mind for success in any area of your choosing. It is true that your input determines your output—better yet—your input *influences* your outcome.

Your thought track has a close relationship with your talk track. Sometimes the conversations that are created within your thoughts are self-sabotaging. Here is an assignment to help stop the cycle or to break the bad habit.

Change Your Talk Track

Assignment: Over the next week, I want you to become more aware of your internal dialogues. Try to distinguish between your normal thinking voice and your critical voice in your mind.

Here's how you'll tell the difference. Sometimes the easiest way is to notice your feelings. Tune in to how you feel. Do you feel encouraged, empowered, and uplifted? Or do you feel discouraged, disabled, and beaten down? Often, when the critical voice is talking, it makes you feel "down." Trace these feelings back to the actual words in your mind, and it will be obvious why you are feeling down. Anyone would feel down if there was an inner voice saying things like, "You're broke and dumb and out of work. You'll never get your act together." Were you thinking about a past event or experience that made you feel down? When you can pinpoint the cause, you change the effect on you. Exercise your power to replace thoughts that don't serve you well.

Once you hear the inner critical voice, tune it down by not agreeing with it. Begin to speak out loud positive words that contradict the negative.

Positive Mental Attitude

A positive attitude takes more than just blocking out the negatives. You must keep your mind in a state of faith. This will keep you mentally and emotionally strong. You will be more likely to be "feeling good" emotionally rather than being down or depressed.

One way to take charge of your thoughts is by literally programming the right thoughts in your mind. This helps get rid of excuses.

Too often, we fill our lives with excuses, which ultimately hinder us from progress. Common excuses are:

- I don't have time.
- I'm too tired.
- I don't have enough money.
- I don't feel like it.
- No one will help me.
- I don't know how.

If you desire to make progress in any area of your life, it's imperative to put excuses behind you for good. Like an old adage states, "Where there is a will, there's a way." When you are faced with a new opportunity or faced with a decision, look for options before totally discarding it.

Exercise: Identify Roadblocks

- Take an index card and make a list of things that have prevented you from having clear vision about what you

want or about what you want to do in any area of your life.
- Make a list of things that have prevented you from pursuing some of your desires.
- Flip each card over and write the words "No More." Over the next days, weeks, or months, you can conquer clear vision and will be pursuing your dreams.

Ways to Develop a Positive Mental Attitude

The Bible tells us to "be ye transformed by the renewing of your mind" (Romans 12:2). Read and meditate (think on and ponder in your heart) on Scriptures that re-enforce what you are believing for.

Two other ideas that help promote positive thoughts: Write down and speak aloud positive affirmations in the *present tense*. Speak them in the *present tense* so that you are speaking those things that are not accomplished as though they already are a reality. As you speak aloud, you are by faith speaking those things into existence. You can speak decrees and declarations over your life. There is life and death in the power of the tongue, so choose to speak life.

Attitude vs Altitude

There are twenty-six letters of the alphabet. If we applied a number to each letter A-Z (A=1, B=2, etc.), then we could assign a numeric value to each letter in the word ATTITUDE. Those numbers would total up to 100. Which means 100% of what you want to do, of what you want to achieve, or of where you want to go in life. **100% is all about your attitude!**

Clarity of Vision

Secondly, *mind your vision* means to *clarify your vision*. Remember the four connection quadrants I shared in chapter

2? You need to find clarity within all the quadrants of your life. For each one of those quadrants, I encourage you to get a piece of paper and start writing down your desires. What goals do you want to accomplish in these four areas?

At the top of the paper, write each of the four quadrants and draw a line in between them to create columns, or use a fresh sheet of paper to list each quadrant. Start off with general goals. What are the short-term personal goals in your life? What tasks can you do today, this week, or this year? What changes do you want to see in the next one to five years? How about long-term goals? Analyze each of the four quadrants. Start with general goals and then go back to write details. These are the tasks you will accomplish to create the life you want.

Mind Your Own Vision

The final, but equally important meaning to *mind your vision* is that you must devote quality time to mind your own vision. Too often, we tend to postpone pursuing our dreams or we place them in the hands of others, hoping for acceptance, approval, or assistance before moving forward. We pour ourselves into fulfilling the dreams of others while our heart longs for fulfillment. So rather than remaining stagnant and in emotional distress, the next step after clarifying your vision through written and visual representation is to create a plan of action.

Creating memorable family vacations has always been a big deal for me, but they require a lot of planning to incorporate activities that are meaningful for each of us. With my husband not working, the biggest challenge I often faced was the budget. My husband would say, "No, there's not enough money to go on vacation," and for a few years, we did not go. But after I transformed my mind and learned to level up my emotional intelligence, my results changed. I began to mind my own vision.

Instead of allowing the word no and financial limitations to restrain us, I began to think about the potential and possibilities. I would ask myself questions like, "How can I create the cash needed to go on vacation?" or "What should we do to prepare for our trip?" As I made plans and took action, things began to fall into place. In many cases, I received a bonus at my job that was used to span the gap, and in some instances, an increased demand for products or services in my business would fill the need. It makes my heart sing to hear my kids talk about the great times we have had on our family vacations. Little miracles showed up to bless us with our hearts' desires.

What vision have you placed on hold? Which dreams or goals have you postponed or keep putting off because of life circumstances? If you desire for those things to become a reality, it's time to do something about it. It's time to own it by taking action to get you there.

Chapter 7: Declare Victory

Declare Victory Over Battles in Your Mind

Finding victory in the battlefield of the mind is vital. Since thought battles are inevitable, we need techniques to overcome them. A few years ago, almost immediately following an event that I hosted, my mind was bombarded with discouraging thoughts about what I should have said or done and about what I should have done differently. I had thoughts about it being a complete waste of my time: "Why are you doing this, it's not really making a difference. Is what you are doing really going to generate the income that you want?" The thoughts went on and on, and they kept coming. I didn't stop them.

Then I started pondering some of those thoughts in my mind and began to agree with those thoughts and started to talk to myself. "Yeah, that's right; what am I thinking? That was a complete waste of my time. Is this really what I want to be doing?" My mind went into a fog. Those thoughts took me from a place of knowing exactly what I wanted to focus on that year to a place of not knowing what I wanted to do at all.

The next morning when I woke up, I felt so down in my spirit and in my emotions. I thought to myself, "I don't like this feeling, and I can't stay here. How can I get myself out of this?" I got busy doing other things, but I couldn't shake the down, sad, lowly feeling. I thought, "This is definitely not good; what is this?" Then I decided to take a nap to see if I could sleep it off. When I awoke, the feeling was still there. I began to encourage myself saying, "You can't stay here." I began to refocus my thoughts on positive things, on gratitude, and on my goals and my desired outcomes. Then I began to feel better. My joy came back, and I felt strength enter into my body and the anxiety left.

Then I realized that I had been hit. I had been attacked by a flood of negative thoughts. I was wounded and knocked down, but I wasn't aware that I had been hit. I also realized that this wasn't the first time that this kind of thought battle had occurred. Here is what I've concluded. Every time you step out to do or try something new, the negative, discouraging thoughts will show up. Every time you step out on faith to take a chance at doing something new or different, where you could make a difference in the lives of others, the thought battle will occur. Then I had an "aha" moment, realizing I needed to sound the alarm because I knew others were having similar experiences. I needed to sound the alarm for all of my comrades to recognize their true enemy.

Your mind is your greatest battlefield. The thoughts that you take in, process, and begin to believe are the weapons that form against you. So, if those types of thoughts are weapons against us, what can we do to bring those thoughts into captivity so that we can have victory? I want to help you learn how to have victory within the battlefield of your mind. It will help you have a better year and help you to continue moving forward on the goals that you have set out to accomplish this year.

2 Corinthians 10:3-5 (KJV) – "For though we walk in the flesh, we do not war after the flesh: (For the weapons of our warfare are not carnal, but mighty through God to the pulling down of strong holds;) Casting down imaginations, and every high thing that exalteth itself against the knowledge of God, and <u>bringing into captivity every thought</u> to the obedience of Christ;"

When you begin to believe those negative thoughts to be true or to be you, that's when you become defeated. You become defeated when you don't fight those thoughts. You are defeated when you begin to meditate on the negative thoughts and allow yourself to stop trying, to stop doing, and to become stagnant. The warning is this: if you allow yourself to go on this way for too long, it will become a way of life for you. Then you will develop a victim mentality.

But we want victory.

VICTORY:

Victors	**V**ictors'
Initiate	**I**ntuition
Creative	**C**aptures
Thoughts (for)	**T**houghts (that are)
Outstanding	**O**ppressive (to)
Results	**R**emove
Yearly	**Y**our (shame, doubt, fear, anxiety, etc.)

V: Are You a Victim or a Victor?

A victim mentality is when a person looks at everything that is happening in their life as being caused by someone or something outside of themselves. You relinquish your ability to control your thoughts and accept whatever comes. When you relinquish your ability to control your thoughts, you become a victim and a prisoner of war in your own mind. When you become a victim, you don't recognize that your thoughts have become your greatest enemy. To step out of this victim mentality, you've got to make a stand and say NO MORE. "I will no longer accept these negative, limiting, degrading, discouraging thoughts..."

A victorious mentality is when one retains their right and ability to control their thoughts. A victor is one who has more of a positive perspective. One who expects to win and puts forth efforts that align with winning.

Author C. JoyBell C. said, "Life is not compassionate toward victims. The trick is not to see yourself as one. It's never too late! I know I've felt like the victim in various situations in my life, but it's never too late for me to realize that it's my responsibility to stand on victorious ground and know that whatever it is I'm experiencing or going through, those are just the clouds rolling by while I stand here on the top of this mountain! This mountain called Victory! The clouds will come and the clouds will go, but the truth is that I'm high up here on this mountaintop that reaches into the sky! I am a victor. I didn't climb up the mountain; I was born on top of it!"

I: Initiative & Intuition

A victor takes the Initiative to consciously control their thoughts, exterminate any defeating thought, and to take action to get things done.

To develop your intuition, you must become more in tune with your feelings in order to recognize why your mood changes.

Intuit - Latin meaning of intuition - ("to look at, consider"), from in ("in, on") + tueri ("to look, watch, guard, see, observe").

You must look *In to It*. Look into what might be causing you to think a certain way; consider your feelings and mood change to see what is the cause or the source. You have to get to the root or to the source to protect yourself from the next attack. When you recognize that your mood or that your countenance has changed from up to down, from happy to sad, or from courage to discouraged, that you have been hit. Either you past experience or your present experience triggered the negative thoughts.

C: Capture Negative Thoughts and Creative Thinking Heals

A victor captures negative thoughts. Stop them in their tracks, don't accept them. Then when you think creative thoughts about your present or future outcomes, you begin to release hope into your situation.

T: Thoughts Become Things

Thoughts in themselves are creative. Thoughts can create and thoughts can destroy. Once a thought is believed, it is provided with the energy source to develop and to become.

O: Overcoming Attitude defeats Oppression and Outstanding Results

A victor's overcoming attitude defeats oppression. Oppression is mental pressure or distress; it is the state of being subject to unjust treatment or control, and prolonged cruel or unjust treatment or control. When you subject yourself to prolonged negative thoughts, you will become oppressed and controlled by those thoughts. As a living witness, I've seen this happen to a family member. Oppression leads to depression. Oppression can lead to your own recession. You can overcome oppression with an overcoming attitude. Outstanding results are what you need to focus your thoughts.

R: Remove the Shame/Guilt/Doubt/Anxiety to get to your desired Results

Remove the shame/guilt/doubt/anxiety from your thinking. Results are influenced and affected by the thoughts that initiate them. It's time to focus on desired results.

Y: Yes, remove the shame, doubt, fear, anxiety, etc.

Victors say yes to remove their shame, doubt, fear, anxiety, etc. They say yes to improved yearly results.

Your mind is the field where the battle takes place. In order to have a strong, sound mind, you must plant good seeds into your field. You must plant positive information into your mind, so that your field can yield good fruit, so that you can bear good thoughts. I am constantly filling my mind with positive, self-help, and information to help me to grow and become better. The stronger your mind, the less time you will stay down when the thought battle comes.

I'll conclude the victim to victor topic with a few powerful points that I learned from the late Jim Rohn:

- Learn how to handle the hard seasons in your life. Don't wish it was easier, wish you were better.
- Learn how to take advantage of opportunities. Take advantage of opportunities to get better.
- Learn how to protect what you've planted or what you've started. Don't give up when the intruders, the doubters, or dream killers come to attack.
- Learn to take full responsibility of what happens to you.

In summary, if you've planted well, and tended to your crops or fields well, you will reap a bountiful harvest.

Declare Victory Over Adversity

Now that we have Victory over the battles that occur in our minds, what about adverse situations that we face from time to time? Is victory over adversity possible? Absolutely!

How Can We Learn from Adversity?

First, we must understand what adverse and adversity mean. Something that is adverse is unfavorable or acting against. It actively opposes your interest or wishes. It is contrary to your welfare. Adversity works in an opposing direction.

You may refer to adversities as disappointments, defeats, delays, setbacks, and unexpected undesirable events. But you can declare victory in the midst of adversity!

Remember that life happens, therefore, you will face challenges. When they come, you can encourage yourself (like King David often did). Speak aloud decrees and affirmation. Refocus your mind on your goals, and keep moving forward. Finally, know that things will happen in the right time, if you don't faint in continuing to do well.

Do Not Get Stuck

Often, we fall into the trap of giving in to fear, especially when we encounter adversity. Fear of the unknown, fear of failing, and fear of rejection are the most common pitfalls. Do not get stuck; take action instead. Have you avoided the first step because you want to know the whole answer before you start? If so, then you are stuck doing nothing because you do not have the whole picture. Just simply step out and do something. You can always make a change, but if you do not move anywhere, then you are going nowhere. You will spend your life stuck in hopelessness rather than minding your vision.

Focusing on what you can do will lead you in the direction you are supposed to go.

I hear from a lot of people who say that they simply do not know what they are supposed to do. They do not know their purpose. And yet, you must start looking for purpose. Begin to do the work to discover what you are passionate about and what you need to do with purpose. Then you can start coming out of the fog and into the life you are meant to live.

A good way to "act now" is by establishing new daily habits, such as:

- Get specific by clearly defining what you want.
- Visualize your goals.
- Affirm your desires.
- Have a daily attitude of gratitude.
- Stay positive, adopt-a-success-minded faith attitude.
- Replace thoughts that contradict your desires with thoughts that affirm what you want.
- Set daily goals or intentions that move you closer to your vision. Stay focused.
- Apply faith by taking steps to complete each goal. Procrastination is not an option.
- Persevere—keep going even when there are setbacks.
- Don't worry about how things will come together

Once you establish the daily habits listed, your thoughts, your words (spoken and written), and your actions should all be in alignment, working in harmony to *mind your vision* and to reward you with astonishing results in your life. Then you are well on your way to transforming your dreams/goals into reality and attaining your heart's desires. And remember to have FAITH (Full Assurance In The Heart). Be fully assured in your heart and mind that your vision will manifest!

FAITH

Full
Assurance
In
The
Heart

CHAPTER 8: GROW IN WISDOM

The Wisdom Effect

Knowledge, skill, and ability may come from different directions, but when applied they merge into wisdom. Knowledge, skill, and ability are all effects of wisdom.

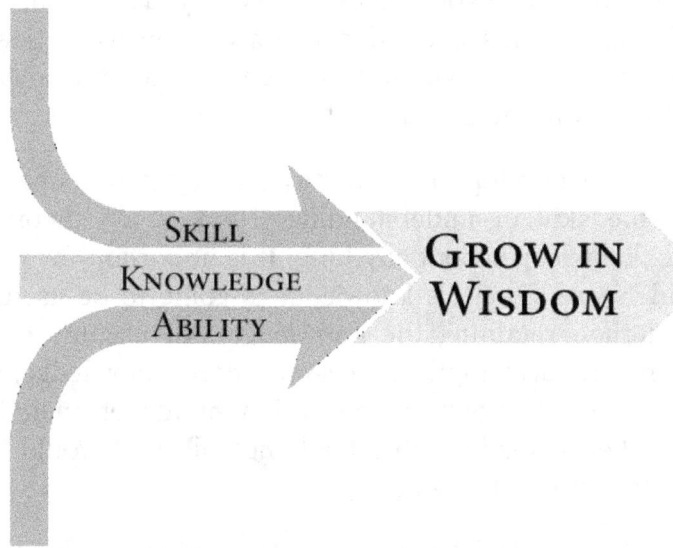

So, what is the Wisdom Effect? Wisdom can affect every aspect of your life. And if you truly understand it, wisdom will inspire you to do great things. Wisdom will give you strategy and offer solutions; it solves problems and brings resolutions. Wisdom is what you pray for when you don't know what to do. Wisdom will give you answers, methods, and means too. Wisdom discerns evil; it is abased (or humbled) so that you may abound (see Philippians 4:12). Wisdom is knowledge with understanding, when at first couldn't be found.

The Wisdom Effect or the Effects of Wisdom:

Let's talk about the word *ability* first. According to Merriam-Webster, ability is "the quality or state of being able, especially: physical, mental or legal power to do something."

The first effect of wisdom is the **ability to apply knowledge, which leads to the skill of understanding.** When you attain knowledge, you have attained some form of information that you acknowledge that you know. Okay, so you have the new information, and you acknowledge that you know this new information. But this new information or knowledge doesn't really become useful to you until you understand how to use it or apply it to your life in some fashion.

So, when you develop your ability to apply knowledge, you develop the skill of understanding. Here is my theory on attaining knowledge about anything. It is important for you to first understand how this knowledge is going to be useful to you, and then retaining the knowledge will become easier. That's why practical application can reinforce knowledge. Had I understood the practical application of higher math like calculus when I was in high school and college, I would have retained the knowledge easier.

I believe that I would be even a better engineer today had I understood the purpose behind a lot of what I was learning while in school. In the field of process control engineering, we use math to determine or to develop process models. In layman terms, those process models will control the equipment to operate at optimum levels to produce quality products at low cost, which ultimately helps the company make more money.

Once you can understand the purpose of the knowledge, then you can apply it wherever it's appropriate at your own discretion. Most students do not retain knowledge because they don't understand it or the purpose behind it.

So, here are some questions that you need to ask yourself if you want to understand the purpose of any knowledge that you are trying to attain.

1. What information am I trying to comprehend?
2. Why is this information important to me?
3. How can I apply this information in my life? Practical application...

If you don't know the answers to those questions, ask yourself the question, "Who knows and understands this information?" Then ask them those three questions.

Proverbs 3:13-18 (ESV), (emphasis mine)

> "Blessed is the one who finds **wisdom**,
> and the one who gets **understanding**,
> for the gain from her is better than gain
> from silver and her profit better than gold.
> She is more precious than jewels,
> and nothing you desire can compare with her.
> **Long life** is in her right hand;
> in her left hand are **riches and honor.**
> Her ways are ways of pleasantness,
> and all her paths are peace."

Another effect of wisdom is that ability to get wealth leads to the skill to prosper. The proper use of knowledge in a craft or trade will open doors of opportunity to create wealth, to get paid an income, or to generate income. Here are some steps to follow:

1. Acknowledge your interest in a craft, skill, or trade and begin to try it out—practice.
2. Learn how to properly use the knowledge to build a skill. The more knowledge you attain in how to better utilize or apply a skill, the better you become, or the more skilled you become at that thing. When you hone your skill and become the best, people will want to pay you for that skill.
3. Practice, practice, practice. Remember the saying: "Good, better, best, never let it rest, until your good becomes better, and your better becomes best."
4. Become a student. Study to show yourself approved (see 2 Timothy 2:15). Study and apply the knowledge through practice to prove that you are interested and that you want to grow to become better or to become the best at that skill.

My son Jamicah has worked at building skill at photography. He studies other famous photographers. He studies the effects of lighting and practices how to properly use lighting in both photography and film. He takes photos every day. He edits photos, and he practices on his friends and family. He has taken hundreds of photos for free; now he is being paid to take photos often. He has been hired to take senior photos, prom photos, military ball photos, glamor shots, music artist album covers, author photos, and more.

When I think of being skillful or skilled at a trade and how it can open doors for you, I think of the following Scripture, where God called for those who were skilled in their craft or trade to build the tabernacle. That means when you become one of the best at applying your skill, you will be called to do great things. You will be recognized as one of the best, and great doors of opportunity will open for you.

Exodus 36:1 (KJV)

"Then wrought Bezaleel and Aholiab, and every wise hearted man, in whom the LORD put wisdom and understanding to know how to work all manner of work for the service of the sanctuary, according to all that the LORD had commanded."

Exodus 36:1 (NLT)

"The LORD has gifted Bezalel, Oholiab, and the other skilled craftsmen with wisdom and ability to perform any task involved in building the sanctuary. Let them construct and furnish the Tabernacle, just as the LORD has commanded."

I believe that everyone reading this book has a skill that can bring you wealth. Sadly enough, though, some people won't attain riches because of how they look at wealth. Some people look at wealth as bad or as something that you shouldn't desire. And they will talk about the rich young ruler who didn't want to give up his wealth when Jesus told him to. When the young man asked how could he inherit eternal life, as he had done everything right in life, then Jesus told him, "One thing you lack: go and sell all you possess and give to the poor, and you will have treasure in heaven; and come, follow Me." (Mark 10:21 NASB). Then, the rich man walked away sad and disappointed.

The one thing that the rich young ruler lacked, in my opinion, is wisdom. Had he understood that he was given the ability to get wealth, he would have understood that even if he gave everything that he had to the poor, to follow Jesus, he could produce wealth again. The same ability possessed to create wealth before could be used throughout his life.

That story tells me wealth without wisdom is worthless. You need both wisdom and wealth to experience true prosperity.

Another effect of wisdom is the ability to discern evil intentions, to discern right from wrong, which leads to the skill of discernment. Wisdom can be considered as a facility of discerning or judging what is most just, proper, and useful. With wisdom you have discretion to exercise sound judgement.

For example, King Solomon showed great wisdom when two women stood before him claiming the same baby (1 Kings 3). How did he know who was the true mother? He used wisdom to discern the evil intentions of the woman who was lying. He used wisdom to discern the truth.

[23] The king said, "This one says, 'My son is alive and your son is dead,' while that one says, 'No! Your son is dead and mine is alive.'"

[24] Then the king said, "Bring me a sword." So they brought a sword for the king. [25] He then gave an order: "Cut the living child in two and give half to one and half to the other."

[26] The woman whose son was alive was deeply moved out of love for her son and said to the king, "Please, my lord, give her the living baby! Don't kill him!"

But the other said, "Neither I nor you shall have him. Cut him in two!"

[27] Then the king gave his ruling: "Give the living baby to the first woman. Do not kill him; she is his mother."

[28] When all Israel heard the verdict the king had given, they held the king in awe, because they saw that he had wisdom from God to administer justice.

Lessons of Four Little Things Upon the Earth that are Exceedingly Wise

Proverbs 30:24-28 shares that there are four small creatures that show great wisdom. We can learn something from each of them.

1. **The Ant**: We learn the wisdom of being mindful of prudence, planning and preparation. "The ants are a people not strong, yet they provide their food in the summer" (Proverbs 30:25 ESV). Ants follow a pheromone scent trail laid by scout ants to gather food. Likewise, we need to use our senses and lay a trail for our children or family to follow. Be mindful and think like the Ant. Think about the future and plan for it. Get in the habit of storing up and saving or investing for the future and pass down those good habits. Be wise beyond your size. Ants are small, yet they are wise. Bank accounts may be small now, but if you begin to understand and apply the principles of investing, your nest egg will grow and outgrow you.

2. **The Conies**: We learn the wisdom of positioning and protection. "The conies are but a feeble folk, yet make they their houses in the rocks" (Proverbs 30:26 KJV). The rocks relative to us are things that provide a solid foundation. The conies are weak, but they build their houses within a solid foundation. How do we secure our homes? We secure our homes through insurances. We must also learn to secure ourselves by learning the financial structures and tax laws to protect the money that we earn. We learn how to position ourselves to protect ourselves. When you position yourself by setting up a business based on the tax laws, the tax laws become a shelter for your money. You keep more of what you earn rather than giving it away in taxes.

3. **The Locusts**: We learn the wisdom of partnering and propagation, which according to Merriam-Webster is "the act or action of propagating: such as increase...in numbers, the spreading of something (such as a belief) abroad or into new regions, an enlargement or extension...in a solid body." Locusts "go they forth all of them by bands." (Proverbs 30:27 KJV). They band together in great numbers. There is power in numbers. When you build partnerships and partner together, each of you can profit or prosper. Biblical math tells us that one can produce one thousand, but two can produce ten thousand, which means that each of the two would have five thousand. Two is better than one.

4. **The Spider** or **the Lizard**: We learn the wisdom of practice, persistence, and prosperity. Proverbs 30:28: "The spider taketh hold with her hands, and in kings' palaces." (KJV) or "The lizard taketh hold with her hands, Yet is she in kings' palaces." (ASV). The spider diligently uses the works of her hands, practices with persistence, and then makes her way into great places. And the lizard has the skill of blending. They blend in with the environment and profit from those who have already established themselves in wealthy places. Likewise, we must use the work of our hands to prosper and learn the art of blending.

Final Thoughts on the Wisdom Effect

The Wisdom Effect will bring you a piece of heaven. You'll have health, harmony, happiness, and your hopes will be fulfilled. You will have hallelujah moments of thanksgiving and hallmark moments that you will always cherish. It will bring you honor and riches. And you will have the heart to help others.

Wisdom will give you strategy and offer solutions,

Wisdom solves problems and brings resolutions,

Wisdom is what you pray for when you don't know what to do,

Wisdom will give you answers, methods, and means too.

Wisdom discerns evil, it is abased so that you may abound,

Wisdom is knowledge with understanding, when at first couldn't be found.

For more great content in audio form, please check out my podcasts at https://mooreofrachel.audioacrobat.com/rss/inside_out_empowerment.xml

CHAPTER 9: POWER-UP YOUR DREAMS

Now that you have your vision and understand the type of mindset required to achieve it, you may start to think about how you will achieve it. Don't worry about the unknown details for now, just stay focused on your vision.

For example, my first invention was a three-year journey. It was not an easy journey, because I was stretched to grow in knowledge to learn the patent process. Rather than retreating, giving up, or just hiring someone else to complete the patent process for me, I stayed in the fire. We are given choices, but we oftentimes choose to get out of the fire because it seems so hard. Those fiery trials are intended to stretch and mold us into new areas of growth. My three-year patent process taught me what not to do when writing your own patent specifications. It was all for a purpose, because I now help others with their patent applications as another means of income, which provides seed money for my other patent-pending invention.

Next is a list of daily habits that helped me stay focused on my vision to be granted my first United States Patent.

Keys to Making Progress Toward Your Vision

- Gratitude: Have an attitude of gratitude every day. Give thanks daily.
- Stay positive and knock out doubt.
- Focus on what you want, not what you don't want.

- Set daily goals or intentions that move you closer to your vision.
- Develop an Action Plan—it can be as simple as creating a To-Do List
- Take action to complete each goal.
- Have perseverance—keep going even when there are setbacks.
- Don't worry about the unknown details, just stay focused on your visions and follow Divine-guidance

Steps to Practicing Daily Visioning

- Step 1: Reflect on the images and power words on your Vision Board (see yourself and feel the joy of achievement)
- Step 2: Decide which goal(s) you want to focus on that day (pray for guidance and direction)
- Step 3: Write down specific action steps you need to take toward those goals
- Step 4: Prioritize your list mentally or with labels
- Step 5: Check off as you complete them
- Step 6: At some point in the day, speak your affirmations in present tense
- Step 7: Capture thoughts, ideas, progress, milestones, and success within your journal

Written Reminders

Achieving or attaining anything in life is much more than setting goals. There will always be various distractions that can slow you down or divert your attention, so having written and visual reminders of those goals can redirect you back to your goals. It's important to translate your goals into realistic daily tasks with target deadlines and milestones. Then follow through with faith and focus by taking action to drive each task to completion.

While doing these steps, it is also important to stay connected to the Source and giver of all good things. Always welcome divine intervention, because it works in our favor. Always be willing to rework or adjust your plans.

Remember, it's your vision. You must believe in it, you've got to own it, and you must take action. It helps to engage your senses. See your vision, feel it, take it for a test drive. Keep track of your progress in your journal.

Assignment

Inside your journal, write down at least one goal or desire for each element of your life. If you struggle with one, move to the next one.

If possible, meet with a family member, friend, or group to discuss at least one of your goals. Ask the person or people you are meeting with to recommend action steps to achieve that goal. Then write down the suggestions and recommendations being made. Offer to share your suggestions for their goals as well.

Affirmations

An affirmation is a declaration that something is true. Affirmations are powerful because, in many cases, you are speaking by faith. You are speaking those things that are not yet as though they already exist. I trust the process of life to bring me my highest good. State aloud your personal affirmations.

Examples of Affirmations

- There is light flooding all around me, helping me to find my way.
- I make a positive wish today, and every day I see a miracle happening in my life.
- Today I have a goal to live tomorrow's dream, for my future depends on me.
- Challenges are opportunities to learn and grow.
- The vision for my life is becoming clearer every day.
- I ask for guidance daily and actively pursue life with passion.

Here are some personalized affirmations with feeling words in them. They connect with your emotions.

- I am so thankful that my life is filled with abundance and wealth (in relationships, health, and money).
- I am feeling delightful and peaceful as I relinquish those things that are out of my control.
- I look and feel great because my body is in excellent shape.
- I will experience daily thoughts and feelings that keep me encouraged and on the right path to achieve my hopes, dreams, and goals.
- I have feelings such as peace, love, joy, order, humility, confidence in my abilities in God's strength, and relaxation.

Assignment:

Write a list of personal affirmations that you can began to declare in your life.

_____

_____

Supporting Scriptures

Psalm 37:4 (ESV): "Delight yourself in the Lord, and he will give you the desires of your heart."

Psalm 21:2 (NIV): "You have granted his heart's desire and have not withheld the request of his lips."

Matthew 21:21 (ESV): "Truly, I say to you, if you have faith and do not doubt, you will not only do what has been done to the fig tree, but even if you say to this mountain, 'Be taken up and thrown into the sea,' it will happen."

Philippians 4:5-8 (ESV): "The Lord is near; do not be anxious about anything, but in everything by prayer and supplication with thanksgiving let your requests be made known to God. And the peace of God, which surpasses all understanding, will guard your hearts and your minds in Christ Jesus. Finally, brothers, whatever is true, whatever is honorable, whatever is just, whatever is pure, whatever is lovely, whatever is commendable, if there is anything worthy of praise, think about these things."

Spring into ACTION

If you want to experience continued satisfaction in meeting your goals in any area of your life, it's time to spring into action on a new level.

You know you need to spring into action if you are not satisfied with the results any area of your life and you want to change or improve those results. Why is *spring into action* important to getting optimal satisfaction? I'm talking about taking the appropriate actions to experience satisfied results.

I was inspired to discuss springing into action after having several new ideas spring into my mind. I immediately wrote down my thoughts, which triggered new thoughts along with some specific action steps to take to get thing moving.

Let's focus on the word SPRING first. What comes to mind when you hear the word spring? Most likely, you immediately think of the spring season. In this section, I will teach two different aspects of the word spring, and how these two different aspects of spring can be relative to you in the getting results in any area of your choosing. They are:

1. Spring in the sense of taking a leap, or to jump into action.
2. Spring, as in the season of spring.

So let's look at the first aspect of the word spring, *taking a leap or to jump into action*. It's all about action. In the physical sense, if you want to add bounce or acceleration to something, you can place spring hardware as a launching device. I think of a trampoline. It has several springs. And the harder you jump, the higher you bounce upward or spring upward.

There is a scientific law that states "for every action, there is an equal and opposite reaction." This scientific law is Newton's third law of physics, and it can be applied to taking a leap or to jump into action. The deeper you dive into task-oriented action to accomplish a goal, the higher you will spring forward or upward toward your desired results.

So it's time to spring into action by taking a leap of faith. Try something new or alter the actions you have been taking to see if your results improve. Do something new or do several small tasks toward that one goal now and watch what happens. For example, one of the new things that I was recently springing into action on is that I was exploring the idea of licensing one of my patents. I would no longer have to manufacture the product, and the company would pay me a royalty fee for using my patent. You should also explore new methods of action that you can take to improve your results. If you are working toward your weight-loss goal, mix up your workout routine or add something new to your workout and see how your results are altered and improved.

Spring into action by taking a leap of faith. Do something with your idea. Like the trampoline with the springs, the deeper you dive or the harder you jump, the higher you will spring forward or upward.

The season of spring is the second aspect that I want to explore. What typically happens in springtime? You have April showers and May flowers. A lot of flowers and trees blossom in the season of spring. The outdoor temperature is warming up to provide the perfect climate for things to spring into bloom.

There are four seasons in a year: spring, summer, autumn and winter. Each season is marked by different weather and hours of daylight. We have seasons because the earth takes a year to move round the sun, which gives us light and warmth, and because the earth tilts at an angle of 23.5 degrees.

Spring and springtime refer to the season, and also to ideas of rebirth, rejuvenation, renewal, resurrection, and regrowth. Many flowering plants bloom this time of year. Quick growth occurs in the springtime because of the warm climates and rain. There are a lot of fruits, vegetables, and herbs that are both grown and harvested in the spring season.

Now how is this relevant to springing into action to get optimum results? There is an equal reaction between the things that occur in the natural and the things that happen in the spiritual. Why do you think that now is the prime time to spring into action? There is a spiritual law of sowing and reaping. Sow in the spirit or in the natural, and you will also reap in the spirit or in the natural.

Thoughts that you have are seeds, and it's up to you as the gardener or farmer to do something with those seeds. How many people actually recognize the thought whenever a new idea pops into their head? How many people actually write down the idea and begin to take some form of action? Here's what to do to grow your seeds when a thought of a new idea comes to mind.

Plant that seed of thought on paper—write the thought about the idea onto paper so that you can refer back to it later. Writing it down allows that thought to take hold and grow. Writing down the thought is a form of action. It's the first form of action that you are taking to help establish that thought or idea in the earth. Thought occurs within our minds, which are intangible realms within the spiritual or non-physical realm. Our minds are the breeding ground for thought. However, thoughts can easily fade away if we don't establish the thought idea into the earth by writing it down.

Now whenever you plant a seed in the natural, what would you do to help the seed to grow? Once you plant it into dirt, and dirt is the earth. Once you plant the seed into the earth, you would probably water the seed, in hopes that it will grow. You would also place your planted seed in a place to get sunlight. The warmth of the sun and the refreshing water both play a big part into the seed sprouting.

In the case of your *seed thought idea* that you want to sprout, you will need sunlight and water as well. An inspiring, warm environment would be considered the sunlight. Your *seed thought idea* will need a warm environment that is conducive to growth, so only share your idea with people who are warm, supportive, and offer you encouragement. And resist sharing it with those who are less supportive, negative, or discouraging. Being around warm, supportive people will inspire you to think outside of the box about your idea, which will inspire new thoughts and actions.

Water does two things to a seed. First, it activates enzymes that stimulate the release of food energy stored during dormancy. Second, it splits the tough seed coat open so that oxygen gets in. Without water, seeds can't use their stored energy. This stored energy only lasts so long. That's why a sprouting seed works so hard to break the soil and unfold into the light quickly. It's also the reason that germination of many seeds is triggered by light. If a small seed germinated in a moist but dark environment, it might run out of energy before ever reaching the soil surface.

But before a seed begins to grow up, it grows down, anchoring itself with a root, the first life to emerge from the seed coat. The root allows the spout to begin to absorb water and nutrients from the soil.

Before our *seed thought ideas* begin to grow up, they must grow down. Before our ideas can spring into reality, they must become rooted deep within our minds. To help with that process, we must first write the thought ideas down. When thoughts become rooted within the mind, they are in position to grow. When we've made up our minds to do something about the thought, that's when it literally takes root in our minds. As it is with the natural seed, the root allows the spout to begin to absorb water and nutrients from the soil.

Here are a few things that are essential to springing into action:

- You need to break the habit of ignoring your thoughts.
- You need to have a plan.
- You need to have an easy process to follow that shows you major steps that should be included in any action plan.
- You need to have a form of inspiration to keep you moving forward.
- You need to establish SMART goals. (Refer to the last chapter.)

Supporting Scriptures:

Isaiah 58:11 (NIV) "The LORD will guide you always; he will satisfy your needs in a sun-scorched land and will strengthen your frame. You will be like a well-watered garden, like a spring whose waters never fail."

Isaiah 44:4 (NIV) "They will spring up like grass in a meadow, like poplar trees by flowing streams."

Isaiah 32:20 (NIV) "How blessed you will be, sowing your seed by every stream, and letting your cattle and donkeys range free."

CHAPTER 10: OWN IT AND CARRY-ON

Own IT and Carry-On

Developing an action plan is where you take ownership; it is where you begin to own IT. When I think of those two words—own it—my mind flashes back to my "journey to close" experience. The long, drawn out process of an extended period to close on a property caused mental exhaustion and fatigue. We were ninety days past the original close date. And on that particular day, I had high hopes to close on the property, but the final piece of paperwork did not arrive at the attorney's office.

After returning home, I lay down for a nap, hoping to clear my mind of the disappointment. Later that evening, going to see a movie became my way of escape. While browsing the list of feature films online, I randomly chose a movie, "Southside with You," and purchased tickets. Then my husband and I were off to the theater.

Shortly after the movie started, I discovered that it was a story about how Barack Obama and Michelle Robinson met and became a couple. The *Southside with You* movie was a nice, short and sweet story about their life well before becoming a First Couple in the White House. During one scene where the character Barack was standing and speaking in front of a group of people at a community center meeting, an unusual thing occurred. The screen appeared to illuminate as Barack admonished the people with the following words: "We've got to stop letting the word NO stop us. NO is just a word. When you turn that word around, it is ON. So let's Carry-ON." Then the crowd repeated, "Let's Carry-ON."

When Barack said the word "ON," the screen illuminated to me. Then, I suddenly recalled a night dream that I had just two nights prior. Within the dream, I saw the words Rachel.ON. My thought while in the dream was that it was somehow connected to the Oprah Winfrey Network, because I saw her face. There were other celebrities in the dream buying domains with their first name.ON, which somehow linked all of their social media. Of course, it didn't make any sense to me at first, so I asked God for understanding and for the meaning of the dream. Then while watching the movie, I received my answer, or at least part of the answer, to the meaning of the dream. It was the scene about turning the word NO around to ON, and to Carry-ON. My answer to Rachel.ON was Rachel, Carry-ON. I was being encouraged not to give up on my journey to close on this property.

After we left the theater, I decided to call my mother to share what happened while watching the movie. I also told her about my Rachel.ON dream. When I mentioned Oprah Winfrey Network, she exclaimed, "That's OWN. ON is OWN." Depending upon your dialect, those two words have similar pronunciations. The significance to the OWN part in this case is that you've got to own IT. You've got to own the responsibility of carrying out what you started. Then, you can celebrate when it's brought to a close.

When I awoke the next morning, the ON experience was still on my heart and in my thoughts. I then began to pray and to ask for more insight about my Carry-ON and journey-to-close experiences. The first part of message was clear. "You are to Carry-ON in doing whatever you've set out to accomplish until the matter is closed. Don't let the word NO stop you, but Carry-ON."

Look at your options and refocus with an OWN-IT attitude. You have to take full responsibility for your part to attain your IT. Seek for answers on what you can do to accomplish that thing that you've set out in your heart to do.

Now, fill in your name: _____.ON, _____, Carry-ON to close the matter.

That same morning, I was reminded of something that someone told me years ago. It became the last bit of insight needed to interpret the full meaning of my dream. I was told that I would become "a people of faith." At that time of my life when those words were spoken, I didn't quite understand it all. Now, here it was, many years later, and those very same words began to resonate in my mind.

Out of curiosity, I decided to search for relevance. I found that everyone described in Hebrews Chapter 11 had great faith. Having read this chapter in the Bible many times, I wasn't expecting to recognize anything new. But when I got to verse 32, I became speechless. The name Barak was listed among other names of people who obtained promises through faith. I then realized that the illuminating screen experience occurred to capture my attention. The name Barak helped to link the words "faith and obtained promises" with the words "carry-on."

It all made sense now. These experiences combined (the Rachel.ON with OWN dream, the Barack movie with Carry-ON, the lesson gleamed from my journey to close experience, and the verse about obtained promises through faith) all basically summed up everything that I've been teaching others:

Through faith, you can obtain promises, the desires of your heart, and live life more abundantly.

By now you might be wondering when I actually closed on the property. One week later after "getting the message," so to speak, the closing for the property was finalized. I was grateful that I didn't give up on the process. I carried on, and now I own IT.

Be encouraged to own your IT. Like the celebrities in my Rachel.ON dream, buy into your own vision and it will pay you great dividends later. Celebrate the life that you desire to live by investing in your future. And get ready to be transformed in the process. You can mind your own vision through applied faith. To do this, you should set aside time daily to work at your vision intensely so it becomes reality. You mind your vision by working your plan.

Another one of my mottos is "A Vision is a Terrible Thing to Waste." The same is true for your time. Use your time wisely and choose to do something each day that supports your vision. Whether your vision or dream-goals include family vacations or something much bigger, your willingness and stick-to-it-ness will determine your outcome.

Fill your day with actions that align with your dream-goals, or at least do something daily that relates to where you want to go in life. We have all been given twenty-four hours in a day. It's totally up to us to choose how we steward our time. If you don't mind your own vision, who else will?

Be persistent and consistent in taking appropriate action toward achieving your dream-goals until you experience success.

Ask yourself the following questions:

- Am I clear on what I want?
- Do I have my vision written out?
- Do I have my dream and goals represented visually?
- Have I developed an action plan or a task list that will move me closer to attaining my vision?
- Have I done anything today that is in alignment with what I desire?
- Do I make the best use of my time each day as it relates to my goals?

Your answer to the above questions will give you a good indication of your Goal Performance Status (GPS). If most of your answers were "yes," then your GPS is high. You are doing productive activity on a consistent basis toward your goals. You are experiencing the taste of victory as you complete the small steps toward attaining your vision. On the other hand, if you answered "no" to most of the questions, your GPS is low. When you think about it, you may feel a bit frustrated because you have not made much progress in attaining your goals.

Because of all the hats that we wear, it is nearly impossible to do everything that we want to do all at once. Choose to set one or two goals at a time as top priorities in each of the four quadrants of your life. Then focus on budgeting time for activity toward those goals. At times, one of the top priorities in a quadrant may take precedence over everything else. You may feel totally out of balance, but that's okay. Adjust by doing whatever you can in the other areas of your life until you have free time to do more. It is important not to become complacent and forget about your priority goals. Reflect on your visual reminder to reassure yourself of your progress, even when your progression is at a much slower pace.

If you have not done so already, it is time to prove to yourself that you are serious about transforming your dreams and goals into reality. Make a conscious decision to put procrastination behind you for good and beef up your GPS. Your decision to do, or to not do, will affect the fulfillment of your vision. The lack of fulfillment can have an adverse effect on your family and others who might otherwise benefit from your life's work on a short-term or long-term basis.

You may be thinking, "Where do I go from here?" Hopefully by now you have a visual aid that reflects what you want. So you carry on by applying the 3 F's: Focus, Faith, and Follow-through. Focus your mental attention on specific outcomes. With faith, believe to receive, and then follow through by putting focus and faith into physical action daily.

Effective Ways to Endure Delays

It is important to carry ON when you are hit with delays. Delays are difficult, but there are effective ways to endure. Some delays are induced by our own means of neglect and distractions, while other delays are caused by external factors that are out of our control, such as the delays I encountered in the real estate closing. In most cases, delay does not mean denial, but it does carry significance. In this section, we will take a deeper dive into understanding delays and explore what to do while you wait.

First of all, let's define delay as the amount of time that a thing or event is late or postponed. If something is late or postponed, that means that it has passed a target date, passed an original due date, or has gone past what you had in mind on your timeline. I'm sure we have all had the thought, "By this time in my life, I want to be here," or "I thought I would be there at this point in my life." We all experience delays on a day-to-day basis. Some things are delayed for months and some are delayed for years. We experience delays on a busy highway when an accident occurs. It can delay us from arriving at a destination at a certain time. We learn to manage those day-to-day type delays, but the difficult delays to deal with are those that extend over a long period of time. Delays that extend over a number of years are the most challenging to endure.

Some delays you can do something about. Some delays you have to wait it out. But, thank goodness, a delay is not a denial. It is only a sign that you need to have peace, patience, and trust that in perfect timing what you desire will come to you. Next, we will explore the different types of delays, potential causes of delays, what to do while you wait during delays, and lastly how to recognize divine delays.

Some difficult delays:

- Waiting to become married
- Waiting to have children
- Waiting to recover completely from an illness, for healing
- Waiting for a promotion that you have worked so hard to get
- Waiting for a financial breakthrough
- Waiting for something that you've lost to be restored
- Waiting for a tough season or a trial/tribulation period to end

All of these difficult delay periods are tough to endure. But the good news is that we can prosper in the process. Just because you are waiting in one area of your life doesn't mean that you cannot prosper in other areas. Unfortunately, some people allow their difficult delays to affect or infect the other areas of their life. How does this happen? Their heart has become sick with discouragement. They become weary during the wait and loose hope.

Proverbs 13:12 (NKJV) says, "Hope deferred makes the heart sick, but when the desire comes, it is a tree of life." Extended delays can cause our heart to become sick, which means that we become discouraged when our desires are delayed over a long period of time. In this sense, our mind, will, and emotions become infected with negative thoughts, sour attitudes, and unhealthy behaviors.

Types of Delays

- **Self-Imposed Delays**: internal factors within your control, such as self-imposed limitations. We limit ourselves with the choices we make. We can choose to do or to not do.
- **External Delays**: external factors beyond your control. Delays caused by other people or other things.
- **Divine Delays:** supernatural factors, sometimes combined with the use of external factors. Divine delays are used to help us to grow, to teach us a lesson, to prepare us so that we are ready when the perfect timing occurs.

What you are waiting for, could be waiting on you.

Internal delays can be caused by our own choices and what we prioritize. They can be caused by fear or procrastination. Staying in our comfort zone with our old routines and methods can also contribute. What you are waiting for, could be waiting on you. External delays can be from complications, issues, problems, or unexpected events.

In getting one of my previous books published, I encountered several things that delayed the publication date. I had to make several editing revisions, then the publishing team and project manager all got sick at the same time. The illnesses delayed the formatting of my book being done for two weeks. Then the book cover design had to be revised several times. Lastly, there were printing issues. These were all external delays. The original date for publication for both the digital version and paperback version of the book was in May of that year. The digital was published in May, but the paperback version of my book was made available in September of that year.

Whenever complications, issues, problems, or unexpected events arise in our life, major delays can occur. But there are steps you can take in the waiting.

What to do during the delays, and while you wait:

- **Breathe through it:** Take a moment to relax and take deep breaths. Refocus your thoughts on what you have right now. Have thoughts of gratitude. As you take deep breaths, focus your thoughts on the blessings that are around you. Sometimes you are so focused on the delays that you tend to forget about your in-the-now blessings. Inhale a deep breath and exhale anxiety. Exhale frustration, release it. Let all of that stuff go. Get it off of your shoulders.
- **Pray through it:** Talk to God about it. Ask for a second wind and the strength to keep you going. Sometimes you can't talk to other people about your issues, but you can talk to God about anything.
- **Sing through it:** There's nothing like singing yourself a song to encourage your soul. When you are feeling anxious or your soul is downcast and discouraged, sing a song. Make up a song and sing. Make a melody to

calm your soul. Encourage yourself with positive self-talk. Speak it into existence in song. When you feel down, that is the best time to sing.

- **See through it:** As hard as it may seem sometimes to believe that your desire will come, you've got to focus your thoughts on the desired end result. See it in your mind.
- **Speak through it:** Speak positive about the process. During the waiting process, find things that are going well in your life and voice it. Even in the midst of the wait, tell yourself what's going well.
- **Share through it:** Confide in wise counsel or in close friendships for strength and encouragement.
- **Plan through it:** Think ahead about next steps, about what else to do while you wait.
- **Grow through it:** Seek for the lesson or message that you need to learn through the process.
- **Give through it:** Occupy your time by giving yourself to others, helping others. Share your story to encourage someone else.
- **Focus on it:** Continue to do your part, focus your actions on working toward that dream or desire. Focus on your *Happy*. What makes you happy? If you don't have an answer to that question, it's time to rediscover your *Happy* again. Maybe your happy is watching a comedy movie or doing your favorite hobby. Whatever it is, doing those things that make you feel happy can help you endure delays.
- **Pursue it:** Don't give up on it. Pursue it and Carry-ON.

Listen to the audio where I share more about *Ways to Endure Delays* at https://mooreofrachel.audioacrobat.com/rss/inside_out_empowerment.xml

Patience is necessary and required in order to endure external delays or divine delays. Waiting forces you to develop patience. It also gives you space to focus on what makes you happy. If you don't know what makes you happy, it's time to discover or rediscover your happy again. Maybe it's watching a comedy movie that makes you laugh or it's doing your favorite hobby that you no longer make time to do.

Sometimes, though, our delay is divinely caused. It may seem hard to figure out if that's the case, but there are some ways to recognize a divine delay. If peculiar activity such as a natural storm comes and delays your plans, that could be divine. Hurricane Irma caused a delay in the start date for the first day of school at SCAD where my twin sons attended as freshmen. Sometimes a physical sign or a wonder is given or occurs to affirm the delay, as in my Carry-ON story.

Also, if you've done all you know to do in a situation, it's likely a divine delay. In cases where you have stepped out in faith by taking actions, you've diligently sought for insight and have followed through with instructions given, and you are still waiting regardless of your effort or prayers, it's a divine delay. Is there a lesson you need to learn, a message you are supposed to get, a stretch you are to feel as you grow in character? These are questions that you should ask yourself.

Within any delay, you should look for the lesson or message. I got the message loud and clear. And almost exactly one year later, I was in a similar delay to my earlier journey to close. I was waiting to close on a property in Savannah. The blessing was that they were able to move in before we closed at no cost to me. So within your delay, look for your blessing.

The Bible has many examples of people acting during a delay. Noah obeyed God in working to build the ark. Joseph prospered along the way during the delay (while he was enslaved and imprisoned) to fulfill his childhood dream of being in authority. And David grew physically (from a child to manhood), and he grew in his gifts and in wisdom between the period of being anointed to be king to actually becoming a king.

Chapter 11: Pursue Passion, Discover Purpose

Discover Purpose in the Process of Pursuing Passion

Everybody can relate to passion. When you have a passion for something, you know it! You enjoy doing it. You may or may not be good at it, but you plan time in your life for it. Passion is realized when you budget time in your life for doing the things you enjoy. Oftentimes passion gets confused with purpose, but there's a distinct difference between the two.

You may have many passions in your life. Every passion does not become your purpose, but every purpose requires passion to pursue it. There must be an element of desire before passion can develop. Desire produces passion. Your mind will say, "I want to do this!"

Your will power will say, "I will do this no matter what!"

Your emotions will say, "I love doing this."

Determination and Will Power=Passion
Passion: Want to do it; will do it; love doing it

This means that you must claim your power. You are not a victim, you are not alone, and you can create the life you want. Stir up your passion for life, and go after it! When you want something bad enough, everything in your soul aligns to work toward the same goal. When you have passion, it will drive you to move forward. Passion is displayed through your determination and will power. Passion becomes the internal drive that motivates your pursuit.

Passion is that internal force that causes you to stay up all night reading a book. It will drive you to practice your favorite sport in the rain. Passion will push you to become the best at what you love to do. Then soon, people will pay you for doing what you love. When that happens, your passion has become a pathway to your provision.

Tell yourself, "My passion has the power to bring me provision."

You may be on a path to discovering your purpose and will find that it is linked to serving other people. Passion becomes the internal drive that motivates your pursuit.

Proverbs 20:5 enlightened my understanding about purpose.

Proverbs 20:5 (NIV) "The purposes of a person's heart are deep waters, but one who has insight draws them out."

We have multi-purposes deep down in our heart and soul, but they will only be discovered if we are insightful enough to seek them out. Since we have multi-purposed lives, I believe that each season of our life unfolds new purpose. Get personal with this area of your life. Define your passions. Define your purpose as you understand it today.

My purpose continues to evolve. In reflection, I have identified two common threads that have been present in every stage or season of my life. As a young girl, I stood on the front porch with paper and pencil in hand, pretending to be a teacher and instructing my little brother. As a teenager, I assisted my home-economics instructor with teaching my classmates sewing basics. After completing college, I pursued my interest in liturgical dance. Then, for over twenty years I ate, slept, and breathed the worship arts ministry of dance. I had a passion for it, I still do, but my purpose in worship dance evolved over the years.

My desire to learn to worship God with thankful heart through dance ignited a passion. Then, I became a student of the art. I started leading and teaching others about worship dance. I helped several churches start their dance ministries. My first book, *Rivers of Praise: Worship through Movement,* was written out of a passion to teach others about creating a lifestyle of worship. Initially, it started with a desire that turned into passion, which lead to purpose. It was no longer about me, but it turned into wanting to help others learn how to worship through movement.

Now, my purpose in teaching others to dance has evolved on a whole different level. For the past decade, I have been teaching others how to "dance with God" in their daily lives. I'm teaching others how to recognize divine guidance, and how to clarify their vision so that they can reach their goals, visions, dreams, and aspirations in a more precise manner. I'm teaching people how to take their ideas and turn them into income. My purpose is to help people become insightful enough to not only draw out the purposes that are within their heart, but to put real plans in place to achieve them. Teaching and inspiring others have been common threads interweaved throughout my life. It's a purpose that I pursue every day.

Manager Moms: Mind Your Vision was written from the perspective of a mom to inspire and encourage women to create the life that they desire, even in the midst of undesirable circumstances. My purpose for this body of work, *Mind Your Vision: 2020 & Beyond,* is to help others cultivate the insight necessary to draw out the purposes in their heart and to create plans to achieve them. Through my products, training programs, books, and empowerment coaching, I am purposefully pursuing my goal to help others turn their dreams and goals into reality.

Purpose is like a seed that is filled with great potential. If the seed is neglected or not watered or nurtured to grow, that potential for what it could become will remain dormant. The seed of great purpose lies within each of us.

We were created with multiple purposes in us, and over the course of our lives, we can live out those purposes. Living out those purposes will occur only if you first discover purpose, and then pursue purpose with passion.

Let me make this clear, every passion does not turn into purpose. When I was growing up, I had a passion for singing. I enjoyed singing, but I did not pursue it to perfect it to serve others. We have multi-purposes deep down in our heart and soul, but they will only be discovered if we are insightful enough to seek them out.

Here are three things your purpose will do:

1. Your purpose will glorify God. Your purpose is always going to be bigger than your budget. Your purpose is bigger than you, but that's where faith comes in. It will require you to grow and to become more.
2. Your purpose will bless you. It will become your provision if you invest your time and your money into you becoming and doing more. It will bless you financially.
3. Your purpose will bless others. Give out of the abundance that is provided through your purpose. Through your purpose, you will serve others through your gifts, talent, skills, and knowledge.

Look Within

Living out your purpose will occur only if you first discover purpose, and then pursue purpose with passion. Many people leave this earth without fulfilling what they were purposed to do. Do not let that be you. Understand that there is more inside of you that has to be drawn out. It is up to you to gain the insight to draw out purpose in every season of your life.

The way we think has a lot to do with how fulfilling our lives are. A mindset of lack will keep you in lack. A mindset of doubt will keep you without. You must change your mind or change the way you think in order to obtain all of the divine promises. It is important to fight the negativity. Do your best to have a positive mental attitude that keeps you in the faith zone. As you master your thoughts and emotions, you will improve your emotional intelligence—a phrase originally coined by two Yale psychologists, John D. Mayer and Peter Salovey.

Psychology Today's website says that "emotional intelligence refers to the ability to identify and manage one's own emotions, as well as the emotions of others. Emotional intelligence is generally said to include three skills: emotional awareness, or the ability to identify and name one's own emotions; the ability to harness those emotions and apply them to tasks like thinking and problem solving; and the ability to manage emotions, which includes both regulating one's own emotions when necessary and helping others to do the same."

This definition of emotional intelligence goes hand in hand with what I discussed in the personal quadrant topic. It's important to look within to become more conscious of how your thoughts influence your emotions and behavior. Once you are consciously aware, then you will attain better control of both your thoughts, your emotions, and of your behavior.

Utilize your emotional intelligence to achieve every purpose that you set out to accomplish.

Your purpose is within; look within your interests and passions, look within your needs, look within your gifts and talents. You can even look within your frustrations. Keep looking, and I'm almost certain that you will discover parts of your purpose along the way.

It will require faith in order to obtain what was intended to provide through living out purpose. It's time to uncover and to discover. It's time to recover or to resurrect. It's time to live life on purpose for purpose. It's your time to pursue purpose with passion. You know that there is more for you. Have you ever had the thought, "I know that there is more to life than what I'm living right now"? It's because **there is more purpose to be drawn out**.

Some of your dreams have become like dry bones; they died on the inside of you because you hoped for so long and they never manifested. The good news is that those dreams can be resurrected. You can give life to those dreams again. Breathe life into your dreams. My *Manifest More of My Dreams* audio training program has all of the elements for you to apply to turn your dreams and goals into reality. This program will help you become more insightful to turning your passion into purpose. More details are listed in the Resources section at the end of the book.

Potential is Essential

Did you know that there is untapped potential dwelling on the inside of you? Your next step is to find out how to discover and develop potential. It's essential to becoming all that you were created to be! It's essential to the fulfillment of your destiny.

You can become more, regardless of your past and present circumstances.

Potential: Capable of becoming reality

Potential is essential to the achievement of your goals and dreams. Potential is essential to the fulfillment of your destiny and living out purpose in your life. So, what is potential? The simple definition in the Merriam-Webster dictionary is that potential is something that can develop or become actual. It means capable of becoming a reality. It may not be your reality right now, but the capability to become is there or is present.

Potential comes from the root words for "potency" and "potent" and refers to all the things you can be successful at if you develop and use your gifts, talents, and natural abilities. Knowing your potential does change your life by helping you understand what you can excel at and who you can become. Knowing your potential allows you to overcome challenges and make your dreams come true.

Your personal potential describes:

- The activities and tasks you can excel at: the hobbies, sports, jobs and relationships you can be great at
- The person you can become: in different professions, social status, and the fame you can attain
- What it is possible for you to achieve: the life goals, wealth, honors, and awards as well as the impact you can have on the world

Look for clues. They are all around you now and may have been there in your past. As a child, you loved specific activities and things. You dreamed of doing great deeds and living a great life. Those dreams and ambitions hold clues about your potential. You are still getting clues now within the things that you love and the tasks you naturally do well without even trying. What places do you feel drawn to? What kinds of things make your heart beat faster when you think about them? What do you dream about and long to do?

Four Ways to Find Hidden Potential

*First, if **desire is present***

When the desire for something new or for something more is present, then you are in a place to discover new potential inside of you. It's time to explore the possibilities. If there is a desire for knowledge or a desire to want to know how to do something, then you are in a position to discover new potential.

*Next, look for your **God-given talents***

What are you already good at? What comes naturally to you? Is it singing, is it carpentry, is it poetry, is it cooking, is it sports? Regardless of what your natural talents are, there is potential for you to get even better and to excel to the point that it financially sustains your family. The things we are intuitively great at, those things that come to us naturally, point to and define our potential.

For example, through my interest to learn liturgical dance, I was presented with the opportunity to choreograph a dance to one song prior to leaving college. At that point is when the desire to worship in the form of dance was born. I enjoyed my first dance experience and wanted to know more. But after graduating and getting married, that desire to dance as worship laid dormant until the next opportunity arose.

*Thirdly, if a **decision concerning you is made by a person in authority or by someone whom you respect***

Certain people can see potential in you before you even recognize that that potential exists. There I was, a recent college graduate and a newlywed moving to the big city of Cincinnati, Ohio, to live with my new husband. We began attending a church in Cincinnati. After a couple of weeks, they were in the process of planning a big birthday celebration for the pastor. During one of the planning sessions, one of the ladies made a statement, "It would so nice if we knew someone who could perform a special dance in celebration of pastor's birthday."

Then I opened my mouth and said, "I've danced once in a liturgical dance." That was it! I was volunteered to dedicate a special dance for the event. After performing the dance that Saturday evening, the pastor came to me and asked if I would start a worship dance ministry for their church. I was flabbergasted! I was thinking, "Me, start a dance ministry, me lead a dance ministry? No way!"

Then months passed, and he asked me the same question again. I prayed for guidance, then I took the leap of faith. I discovered amazing potential that I never knew existed! That pastor saw potential in me. He saw the potential for me to not only dance, but he saw the potential for me to be a leader. I became a student of the trade. I took formal dance classes (ballet, jazz, and modern). I traveled from city to city to attend dance conferences. I began to sew dance garments and props.

After three years, my husband and I relocated to Macon, Georgia. Before leaving, I was the leader of a full-blown worship arts ministry with dancers of all ages, a mime team, and a drill team. I helped churches all over the middle Georgia area to establish dance ministries. That great potential inside of me revealed one of my God-given talents to not only dance, but to teach others to do the same. In 2004, my first book, *Rivers of Praise - Worship through Movement* was published.

I also wrote a song called "Rivers of Praise" and had it produced. While writing my first book, I discovered more potential, the ability to write and author books, which I love to do now.

*Finally, **delays and disappointments** can reveal your potential*

When you want something bad enough, delays or disappointments will drive you to search for options or for other opportunities. Through your searching or research, you might just begin to grow in knowledge and learn what not to do next time, or learn how to do something that you weren't educated or skilled at before the delay or the disappointment.

One example that comes to mind is when I went through the patent application process for my inventions. I experienced a lot of delays and disappointments, but it caused me to dig in deeper and to learn the legal lingo and verbiage. It caused me to dig in and learn the technicalities of applying for patents. I discovered and developed potential that I never knew existed. Had I not experienced the delays or disappointments, that potential could possibly still lay dormant today. Through that knowledge and skill, I have helped several others complete their patent applications through the services that I provide.

In both examples about the dance and about the patent applications, my potential became reality. It's no longer potential, but it is true skill and knowledge.

Develop Your Potential

You develop your potential by doing something. Potential can never be developed if it's static or sitting and resting. Like potential energy is the energy possessed within an object because of its position, stresses, electric charge or other factors, there is potential energy resting dormant on the inside of you. This potential energy is waiting to be awakened by desire. It's within your body. And it's based on your position, whether you are for something or against something, or whether you want something bad enough or don't really care. Desire can ignite an electric charge on the inside of you to turn potential energy into true skill and ability. Doing something to build a skill or to build knowledge helps to develop potential.

Demonstrate Your Potential

Put your skills, your knowledge, and ability to the test. Utilize it to help others. Utilize it at home, at work, in business, or at places where you serve or volunteer. Welcome opportunities to demonstrate your potential.

For several years, I had a desire to become the leader/manager of the process control team at work. The position became vacant in March 2013. I wanted to fill that position, but I had to demonstrate my potential. I had to work my butt off for eight months before my boss offered the position to me. I stepped up to the plate and took responsibility for the success of a $4.5 million controls project. I had to function in about three different types of roles: project manager, process control engineer, and team leader. God gave me the strength, and we pulled it off. The project was super successful, and that November I received my promotion and desired salary request. As I write this book, I now manage even larger projects and a larger team.

You have to demonstrate your capabilities to become more. You may walk in doing a position long before you actually carry the title. Don't allow not having the title stop you from doing and achieving your dream or goal. Just demonstrate your potential and the title will follow.

The original *Karate Kid* movie is another example I think about when it comes to discovering, developing, and demonstrating potential. Mr. Miyagi teaches Daniel to become the karate kid. He helped Daniel develop his skills during the wax-on, wax-off movements while hand waxing the floor. Mr. Miyagi had Daniel do a lot of repetitive motions until they became a natural part of him. Potential is all about becoming more. Potential is all about unlocking possibilities!

Requirements to Becoming More

- Be willing to accept the feelings of inadequacy
- Be willing to fail
- Be willing to learn from your mistakes
- Be willing to commit to a challenge until complete
- Be willing to dedicate a lot of your time toward the development of it
- Be willing to sacrifice

CHAPTER 12: *FAITH IT* UNTIL YOU MAKE IT

You are Not Alone in the Faith Zone

Faith is the mystery behind manifestation. Faith is a spiritual principle supported by spiritual laws. Principles must be applied for faith to work for you. Did you know that faith without work is null and void? Faith will work for you when you learn to work your IT. To apply your faith means to take some form of action toward achieving your goals. You must take appropriate actions that are aligned with your dreams. Be ready to respond to new opportunities that are relevant to your vision.

Applied faith activates both spiritual and universal laws to work in your favor. Let me further explain as it relates to attaining your heart's desires. Whenever you apply faith through your actions and belief of the possibilities, faith becomes the substance of what you are hoping to receive; you hold on to that belief, whether big or small, until your hopes manifest into tangible form. In the midst of your circumstances, you must mentally hold on to your desired outcome by keeping your mind set on believing while blocking out doubtful thoughts.

When you apply faith in any area of your life, you are in the "faith zone." As you function in the "faith zone," you are not working alone, as God intervenes on your behalf. A chain reaction of events can take place just because of active faith. Literally, people, resources, and opportunities for your good begin to just show up in your space.

Since 2010, I have become a student and teacher of active faith and visioning. Active faith is when you believe, pray, and take some form of action toward your desired hope. Active faith is when you continue the course until you are faced with the word no, but you choose not to quit. Active faith is when adversity causes you to retreat for a moment, but you reevaluate the situation and pray for wisdom on the next steps. Active faith is when you carry on in hope while keeping your mind's eye on the desired outcome.

On the contrary, however, oftentimes I've noticed that people demonstrate passive faith through their behaviors rather than active faith. For instance, some people might just pray and wait. They choose to do the obvious or may choose to do nothing at all and passively wait to see what happens. Passive faith is when you want something to happen, but you do nothing toward attaining that desire. When faced with the word no, passive faith retreats. Then their desires become hopes that are never fulfilled.

Exercise Your Faith

One time, I saw the animated movie *Zootopia*, which demonstrated many of the points that I cover in my writing. A young, petite female was the main character in the movie. She had a big dream. She wanted to leave the farm country to go live in the big city and become a key player in law enforcement. When she told her parents about her big dream, they tried to be supportive, but because of their own experiences, their words were not so encouraging.

Her dad responded, "Oh honey, it's nice to have big dreams, but you are just a farm girl. You need to be like the rest of us, honey, become complacent and those big dreams will just fade away. And you just let life be. Isn't that right, honey?" He directed that question to his wife.

But the young girl responded, "No, I know what I want. I'm going to be on the law enforcement team in the big city." She was positive, enthusiastic, and determined to make her big dream a reality. She sprang into action and went off to the city to pursue her dream. The first challenge she had to complete was boot camp. She had to pass the boot camp test before she could become a member of the law enforcement team. It was a tough challenge. She faced all kinds of obstacles. She had to plow through the mud, and she was knocked down several times, but it only made her tougher. She demonstrated what to do when adversity meets persistence. She did not quit, but she wised up.

Then, she began to execute the wisdom effect, which worked like a charm in her favor. She implemented new strategies and learned how to use others as a springboard to excel. As a result, she passed the test and became a member of the team. That was her first victory! Everything that the young girl did throughout the movie fits the topic of exercising your faith. There is a whole lot more to the story, but you'll have to check out *Zootopia* for yourself. You'll enjoy it. It's a cute, animated film with a big message.

So what is faith anyway and what does "exercise your faith" really mean?

Faith is the intangible substance that brings tangible results. Faith is the evidence of things not yet seen in the physical realm, and it is what's necessary to please I AM (that is, God). Faith is what you need working in every situation. It is the powerful force that stirs anticipation.

Faith will move mountains and even cast them into the sea; but only if you believe in the possibility. So believe and don't doubt, because faith works when you work it. It will give you courage when you feel like copping out.

Faith increases revelation. It is the secret antidote that accompanies expectations. And faith anchors you to amazing grace and causes a supernatural transformation to take place.

The Principle of Faith

Apply the principle of faith in your life daily. That's applied faith.

Learn to master the principle in small things in life, then the big will surely come.

In order to embrace the larger purpose when it is revealed, you must first embrace all the other things that came before it.

Things you're hoping for contain a substance or the most vital part that is essential to having those things come true. That substance is called faith. The principle of faith encompasses gratitude, vision, asking, believing, receiving, and giving back.

As Hebrews 11:1 reminds us, faith is the substance of things hoped for and the evidence of things not seen (in the natural or not yet manifested in the natural). In order achieve vision, we must be people with pro-active faith.

And we must be people of action as well. People who plan action steps toward their goals, execute those action steps, evaluate and check for progress. Then revise their plan as needed.

People of pro-active faith look at life through their vision glasses. They see the dream, the end result of a dream or achieved goal. They see opportunities in the place of obstacles. They find courage and confidence to overcome a challenge. They seek God daily for direction and wisdom. They keep their mind in a state of faith. You can be a person like that!

Hebrews 11:6 NIV "Without faith it is impossible to please God."

Faith without works (application) is dead. (see James 2).

If you believe and doubt not, you can have what you say. (see Mark 11:23).

How Faith Works

Faith without Works is Dead = Faith without Actions is Dead

Our works are the actions that we are doing toward a desired outcome or goal. So one way to exercise your faith is to do some form of action to get a desired outcome. I'm not talking about doing something or doing certain actions only one time or a few times. You've got to keep doing and keep taking some form of action until the desired outcome manifests into physical form.

Faith with Works is Life = Give Life to Your Dreams

One single action may not yield your desired results, but you can count it as a part of your works. The more actions you take or the more works you do, they will add up into a body of works that will eventually begin to get results for you. That body of work will take on a life of its own and no longer require as much of your time and effort.

Here's an example of giving life to your dreams through works of faith. When I was inspired with the portable vision board idea in 2009, which is now called Tote-a-Vision, my first goal was to teach my sons how to visualize their desires and set goals. Then my goal became teaching others how to use the Tote-a-Vision as a faith tool to get desired results in their life.

Eventually, my goal evolved into a desire to teach others how to turn their dreams and goals into reality.

In a simplified form, here are some of the works or actions that I have taken toward the manifestation of that desired outcome.

- Turned the idea in my mind into an invention by creating prototypes of my idea. My family and I began to use them and get results.
- Went through the process to receive an official United States Utility Patent.
- Began to teach visualization and faith-building techniques with Tote-a-Vision and dream-building workshops. Those teachings and techniques turned into works of writings, which became workbooks and books.
- Developed a seven-day mini-course to help people get out of a rut and start living the life of their dreams. I am now giving that course away for FREE. The mini-course is available online at

   https://mindyourvision.com/free-resources/.
- Created the "Manifest More" audio training course.
- Started Inside- Out Empowerment Calls. Inside Out Empowerment episodes are now available on WomensRadio.com and as a podcast. The podcasts are available here:
   https://mooreofrachel.audioacrobat.com/rss/inside_out_empowerment.xml
- Published Podcast - Inside Out Empowerment with Rachel
- Published book to provide teachings to everyone who reads it.

In that example, I only highlighted a few things, but over the past several years, I have been consistent in taking some form of action, which has built, or is building, a body of work that will eventually have a life of its own. One day, that body of work will be able to work for me instead of me working for it, which will be a reward for exercising my faith long enough to give it life and to keep it alive. The body of work becomes the evidence of your faith.

It is stated in James 2:18 that you can demonstrate your faith by your works. It's up to you to breathe life into your dreams. Remember, Faith with Works is Life. Exercising your faith is what gives life to your dreams. Let's compare exercising your faith with physical exercise.

Faith with Works is Life.
Exercising your faith is what gives life to your dreams.

If you're going to be physically exercising for more than a few minutes, your body needs to get oxygen to the muscles; otherwise, the muscles will stop working. Just how much oxygen your muscles will use depends on two processes: getting blood to the muscles and extracting oxygen from the blood into the muscle tissue. Your working muscles can take more oxygen out of the blood stream than your resting muscles.

The key components to physical exercise are:

- Muscles - exercise works our muscles
- Oxygen - our muscles need oxygen in order to work
- Blood flow - the only way to get oxygen to our muscles is through the blood flowing to them

The more you work your muscles in exercise, the stronger your muscles become, and the more muscles you will build. To put it all together, exercise is a form of action that works our muscles. As we work our muscles, blood flow increases to provide oxygen to the muscles.

Now, let's compare that to exercising our faith:

1. Muscles = Faith - We have to exercise our faith muscle. We have to work our faith. So if exercise is a form of action, we have to take some form of action to exercise our faith.
2. Oxygen = Breathe - We have to breathe life by speaking those things that are not yet seen as though they were already manifested in physical form. Faith enters the heart of your soul (mind, will, and emotions) through the passageway of your ears. Speaking those things aloud gives life to your desirable outcome.
3. Blood = Sweat and tears that comes from doing work, or that come with taking action

It's not good to separate the two; oxygen needs blood to get to the muscles, and the blood needs oxygen to fuel the muscles. Likewise, to have oxygen-enriched blood that fuels your faith muscles, you have to exercise our faith, through believing, speaking, and affirming that belief with consistent actions.

Faith is powerful! We were all born with a measure of faith. And if we exercise our faith, that measure will grow and increase. We will then you will have the ability to believe for greater things and for BIGGER outcomes!

Forms of "Faith-Ercise" to Exercise Your Faith

Faith-Ercise to attain the prize! Here are some ideas to get you started.

1. Walking: Walk by faith and not by sight. You must believe and not doubt. Doubt is formed by what you see happening in the physical realm around you. Follow

the path of your vision within your mind's eye. You've got to walk this thing out. Don't allow your walk to be altered by distractions, doubt, delays, discouragement, and difficulties. Allow hope and belief to light your path.

Isaiah 40:31 (KJV) "But they that wait upon the LORD shall renew their strength; they shall mount up with wings as eagles; they shall run, and not be weary; and they shall walk, and not faint."

2. Running: Run and not be weary; walk and not faint. Don't become weary and give up. You've got to keep running. Run as if you are in a race toward the prize and get your desired outcome. Exercise self-control to do the necessary things, tasks, or actions.

    Plan and prepare. To avoid running aimlessly, you must create a plan of action. Each day, have a plan of action.

    Discipline your body and keep it under control to do the works of faith toward your goal; otherwise, you might disqualify yourself from attaining the prize.

3. Swimming: Launch out into the deep waters and swim! Test your idea, try that new thing—just do it! The turbulent waters may come to shake you at your core; and the waves may come to seemingly overtake you, but just keep swimming in the direction of your dreams, because the next big wave could launch you forward and take you exactly where you desire to go.

4. Dancing: It's important to learn how to dance in life and allow Divine Guidance to order each step that you take in life. Listen with your heart and flow with your actions.

5. Weight training: Lifting weights adds muscle to your body faster than any other form of exercise. Weightlifting is strength training. Consider our burdens being relative to weights that strengthen our faith. Whenever burdens weigh you down, you have to push and press through; otherwise, you will be buried under the weight. As you push those burdens up to God, who is a higher source of comfort, you've learned to master the spiritual aspect of weight training to build your faith muscle. When you cast those burdens over to God through prayer, you will be sustained and your faith will be stronger because of lifting up that burden to a higher source.

Another important lesson is in active faith to stay attentive to avoid complacency.

Complacency, as mentioned in the Zootopia story, will cause your dreams to fade. When you just settle with life and live your life aimlessly, you are literally giving up on your big dreams. Just because the majority of people around you have become complacent doesn't mean that you have to do the same. Challenge your faith by pursuing your vision, dreams, and goals. It's time to shift from aimlessly living life to faithfully pursuing life on purpose for purpose.

Will it be easy? Maybe, maybe not. But based on my personal experience, living life on purpose for purpose has its challenges. There will be obstacles to overcome, but face them head on. There will be delays to endure, and there will be difficulties and disappointments too. But if you faint not in your mind, will, and emotions—meaning you don't give up—and you exercise your faith, you will prosper. Some things take an extended period of time to be fulfilled. From a biblical perspective, King David had to wait thirteen years between being anointed to be king and his actual appointing to be crowned as king. It took thirteen years for Joseph's dream to be fulfilled. I like the way one of my business mentors, Myron, puts it; he says, "An anointing is for an appointing, but the years in between the two are years of disappointing."

Just remember, even though the vision tarries, wait for it and faithfully work toward it, and it will surely come to pass at the appointed time. When God sees your works of faith, He is moved with compassion to line up things in the Universe to work in your favor. Your faith moves God, then God moves for you!

Here's a poem that I wrote that describes how certain things can affect your faith. In the poem, the word "IT" refers to the word faith.

"Faith is IT from A to Z"

Anger Annoys IT; Affirmations Add to IT

Bad Company holds IT back; Belief Boosts IT

Complacency Shrinks IT; Creativity Expands IT

Doubt Kills IT; but Desire gives IT life

Error Confuses IT; Excitement Energizes IT

Fear Intimidates IT; Favor makes IT Shine

Greed Corrupts IT, Guidance Gives Light to IT

Hope Deferred makes IT sick, but Hope Revived Resurrects IT

Idolatry Taints IT; Imagination Increases IT

Junk Pollutes IT; Joy Strengthens IT

Kingdoms of Darkness War against IT; but Knowledge and Understanding Applied, Win with IT

Lies Limit IT; Love Secures IT

Malice Harms IT; Mercy Strengthens IT

Negativity Negates IT; New Vision Empowers IT

Oversight Overlooks IT; Opportunity Opens Doors for IT

Poverty Mentality Lacks IT; Prayer Partners with IT

Quitting Cancels IT; Quality Actions Accelerate IT

Rocky Waters Trouble IT; Refreshing Rain Waters IT

Stress Exhausts IT; Sacrifice Solidifies IT

Temperance Tames IT; Time Tests IT

Unfilled Dreams Dims IT, but Understanding Your Purpose Ignites IT

Victim Mentalities Trap IT; Victory Triumphs with IT

Worry Upsets IT; Waiting is a Witness for IT

X-Cuses Deny IT, but Your X-Factor Sets IT apart

Yearning Pulls on IT, and Your Soul Controls IT

Zigzagging Confuses IT; Zealousness Motivates IT

Well, that's IT—all about Faith, from A to Z.

CHAPTER 13: PREVAIL OVER DOUBT

It always amazes me how things just show up seemingly out of nowhere to reaffirm your cause, your mission, or your purpose. While finishing up a meal at a Japanese restaurant one Father's Day with my family, the waitress placed a plate of fortune cookies on our table. Each person took a fortune cookie from the plate. When there was only one left, I picked it up, broke it open, and pulled out the slip of paper. "He who believes is strong; he who doubts is weak" were the words written in blue ink. This small quote was a strong affirmation toward the foundation of my teachings regarding transforming your dreams and goals into reality. Those things that we envision for our lives or those things that our hearts long to manifest in our lives will only come about if we believe that it's possible.

He who believes is strong; he who doubts is weak.
– Louisa May Alcott

That little quote about doubt is what inspired me to write this teaching on ways to prevail over doubt. My heart became burdened with the fact that so many people are without because of doubt. You may want things to be a certain way in your life, but you have doubt that it will ever be. Do you desire to manifest more of your dreams, desires, or dream life into reality? Beware of doubt, because it slips in and can destroy your hopes and dreams.

It's natural for us to doubt, but we can't allow it to beset us or to get the best of us. Doubt is something that is formed within our minds based on unfavorable past experiences, from negative conversations with others, from uncertainty, or from the fear of an undesirable outcome.

Doubt is usually the first thing that shows up when there is uncertainty, a challenge, or when fear of an undesirable outcome is present. Doubt saps your strength, drains your energy, and causes you to give up before your big win. Doubt weakens your results and can sabotage your dreams from becoming a reality.

But, there is hope. Belief is our greatest weapon to combat doubt. When your belief is strong, you fuel the manifestation of your IT into reality. When your belief is strong, you fuel the possibilities.

Six Ways to Prevail Over Doubt

1. Stay Focused on Your Goal: Keep your head up. Keep your mind focused on where you want to go, rather than holding your head down in discouragement. Try not to use your current circumstances as a measure of success.

When my then-18-year-old twin sons graduated from high school, they took a trip to Alaska. They were living out one of their dreams. During our family visioning day back in January that year, they both voiced their desire to travel to Alaska with a couple of friends as their high school senior trip. At first, my thoughts were: "I haven't even been to Alaska, you all must be kidding!" and "That's an expensive request." My thoughts about the cost of sending two teenagers on a trip to Alaska was starting to produce doubt as to whether they would go on that trip or not.

To stop the doubt cycle that was going on in my mind, I had to immediately shift my thoughts to agree with them. After all, I had taught them to dream BIG. Now I had to dream big with them and for them. I couldn't allow any doubts to get in their way. Regardless of all the other expenses that came along with them being seniors in high school and the cost for college that shortly followed, we had to believe that their Alaska trip would manifest. We made Alaska a big focus on our family Tote-a-Vision board that year, and they each placed images and words with Alaska on their personal TAV boards.

Jamicah and Jeremy's dream trip to Alaska became a reality, and they will have those moments to cherish forever. Lastly, to top everything off, that fall the twins began attending the college of their dreams.

Our Tote-a-Vision boards helped us to stay focused on the goals that we set out to accomplish that year. The Tote-a-Vision is a visual tool to remind you to mentally focus on your goals. For instance, when you look through a camera lens and you adjust your lens to focus on something that is at a distance, those things close up will become blurred, but the thing that is far away in distance appears closer and becomes clear. The same is true about doubt and your goals. When you began to mentally focus on your goals (either short-term or long-term goals), the doubt of them becoming a reality becomes a blur and that desired reality draws near to you.

When you are taking action, doubtful thoughts become less of a distraction.

2. **Put Your Faith in Action:** If you truly believe that IT is something that you really want, then it's up to you to take some forms of action. Whether your IT is a dream vacation, a new lifestyle, a fit body, a loving relationship, a new job, a new home, or even attending your dream school, whatever your IT

is, the fact remains the same. You must put your faith in action in order to attain IT. You must take action steps toward the achievement of your desire. When you are taking action, doubtful thoughts become less of a distraction. You become more energized because you experience progress towards your IT.

In the case of my twin sons' desire to attend their dream school, we all had to put our faith in action. The college cost around $60,000 per year, per student, to attend, which includes tuition, room and board, and meals. Three years prior, my oldest son wanted to attend the same school, but I allowed doubt to hinder me from action to make that dream possible. He did his part in working hard in school to get academic scholarships. But I allowed negative conversations with others regarding the cost being too high, and I allowed the thoughts of getting in a lot of debt to become my focus. As parents, we can either become the barrier to our children's dreams or we can breathe life into their dreams. Through that experience, I saw the flame of passion for his craft in animation and film go dim. It was disheartening to watch, but thankfully it lasted only for a short season.

After witnessing what happened to him, I became determined to no longer allow the negativity from others to influence destiny for me or for my children. My oldest son ended up going to a local university for a few years. Then he expressed to me his desire to attend Georgia State University in Atlanta. I went into full action mode. Jonathan has a place in Atlanta and is pursuing his dreams. That flame for film and animation rekindled. He has a major in Computer Science and a Minor in Film.

Mathew 7:7 "Ask, and it will be given to you; seek, and you will find; knock, and it will be opened to you. **8** For everyone who asks receives, and the one who seeks finds, and to the one who knocks it will be opened. (ESV)

3. **Apply the Ask, Seek, Knock Principle:** To give yourself confidence over doubt, your faith in action must be coupled with prayer and trust in a higher source who is working in your favor. Just knowing that God is working in the background on your behalf makes doubt diminish. Prayer is simply a conversation with God. You make your desires known, and then ask to receive those things in your life. You ask in faith, believing that you will receive. You ask for His guidance to help you seek out the right opportunities that will get you closer to your goal. Then you knock on the door of opportunity by taking some form of action. Partner with God and believe that He will work on your behalf.

For instance, when I was uncertain about where all of my sons would stay while away from home at college, I asked God for guidance. I was inspired to seek out real estate opportunities. Then as I knocked on the doors of different properties, eventually the right door opened for me.

As a family we saw really neat things happen, as we prevailed over doubt.

Supporting Scriptures:

Luke 11:10 (ESV): "For everyone who asks receives, and the one who seeks finds, and to the one who knocks it will be opened."

Matthew 7:7 (ESV): "Ask, and it will be given to you; seek, and you will find; knock, and it will be opened to you."

James 1:6 (ESV): "But let him ask in faith, with no doubting, for the one who doubts is like a wave of the sea that is driven and tossed by the wind."

Mark 11:22-24 (ESV) (emphasis mine): "And Jesus answered them, 'Have faith in God. Truly, I say to you, whoever says to this mountain, "Be taken up and thrown into the sea," and <u>does not doubt in his heart, but believes that what he says will come to pass</u>, it will be done for him. Therefore I tell you, whatever you ask in prayer, believe that you have received it, and it will be yours.'"

Mark 10:27 (ESV): "With man it is impossible, but not with God. For all things are possible with God."

So remember to:

Ask in faith; Seek for guidance, insight, knowledge and understanding; then Knock with wisdom and determination toward the fulfillment of your dream.

4. **Trust Your Decisions:** Whether it be personal related, business related, or ministry related, you must trust your decisions. Especially if you have already asked for divine guidance and insight. If you have already taken the necessary steps to assist you in making a sound decision, then trust your decision, and don't allow others to cause you to doubt.

Once at work, I had an internal candidate who applied for two different positions that I had open. I observed the candidate's answers and interaction with the interview panel. Afterward, it was decided that the individual wasn't quite ready for either of the positions, but that they should be given an opportunity to be developed. I was later questioned by two different members on my team about my decision. Since I respected their opinions, I began to question and even doubt my decision. As soon as I began to doubt, I lost my inner peace about the situation. I was allowing their questions to drive me to change my decision. I was being tossed by the wind of adversity.

After speaking with two members of leadership regarding my initial decision, I was advised not to question my decision and not to go back on my decision. As soon as I shifted my thoughts back to my original decision, my inner peace returned. That inner peace was my true guidance to let me know that I was going in the right direction. Both groups gave sound advice, but the one thing that confirmed to me that I was headed in the right direction was the inner peace. A few days later, another leader came to me to tell me that they had plans for the individual who had interviewed. Absolutely everything worked out for good.

5. **Follow the Way of Peace:** Follow the inner peace within your belly. Some people say *go with your gut*, but the spirit part of your being resides within your inner core. When you are in doubt, take a few minutes to tune in to determine if you have peace within about a certain situation or direction.

6. **Patiently Wait on the Vision to Manifest:** The desire, the dream, the vision, or that which you hope for to manifest, you have to patiently wait on it. Trust that God has divine timing for it to manifest.

Romans 8:25 (ESV): "But if we hope for what we do not see, we wait for it with patience."

Habakkuk 2:3 (ESV): "For still the vision awaits its appointed time ... wait for it; it will surely come; it will not delay."

A mindset of lack will keep you in lack.

A mindset of doubt will keep you without.

Finally, it is good to meditate on scriptures about faith. See Matthew 17:20; Romans 10:17; Matthew 21:21; and James 1:6.

Help My Unbelief

I know that believing for something and not doubting that it will ever become a reality, is a lot easier said than done, because it's in our human nature to doubt. Another very simple and direct way to deal with doubt is to face it head on.

There is a story in the Bible about a father who had to combat doubt on behalf of his son (Mark 9:14-29). From childhood, the boy was vexed with a tormenting spirit and no one in his family or local community could help him. This spirit literally tried to destroy the child by throwing him into fire or into water to drown him. The father was extremely burdened that he didn't know how to stop these horrible things from happening to his son. But, one day the father of the boy was told that Jesus was coming to town. This brought great hope to the father because he had heard that Jesus had helped many people in difficult situations.

As soon as the father and the boy were in the presence of Jesus, the tormenting spirit became alarmed and began to convulse the boy; he fell on the ground, rolled around, and foamed at the mouth. "And Jesus asked his father, 'How long has this been happening to him?' And he said, 'From childhood'" (v. 21 ESV). Then the father pleaded, "If you can do anything, have compassion on us and help us." (v. 22 ESV).

Jesus's response was profound: "And Jesus said to him, 'If you can'! All things are possible for one who believes.' Immediately the father of the child cried out, 'I believe; help my unbelief!'" (Mark 9:23-24 ESV).

The most powerful thing about this story is when Jesus answered with "'If you can'! All things are possible for one who believes." Jesus immediately turned the authority and responsibility for the boy's healing back over to the father and reminded him that all he had to do was believe.

In the father's response, he first confessed that he believed that his son could be healed or delivered. Then he admitted that he had his doubts and needed help with his unbelief. Likewise, when you have doubts and unbelief, you need to ask God for help by simply saying, "Lord, help my unbelief."

Sometimes, like that father, things have been a certain way for so long that you lose hope for things to get better, or you've waited so long for something to be that you lose hope. Just remember, God has the power to help you with anything, but it is up to you to first believe that it's possible. Then, ask for help to remove your doubts.

Attaining your goal, dream, or vision is in your hands. Living out your purpose and destiny is in your hands. Your desire to live a happy fulfilled life is in your hands. The key is to believe. Ask God to help your unbelief to prevail over doubt. It is okay to doubt at the start, but don't let that stop you. Do something to move forward and leave doubt behind.

"I had as many doubts as anyone else. Standing on the starting line, we are all cowards."
– Alberto Salazar, 3-time winner of the NYC marathon

Chapter 14: Personify Persistence

With anything that is worth having or doing, there will be some measure of resistance between you and that thing that you want to be, to do, or to have. The ideas that you have are worth pursuing. The dreams and goals that you have can be attained, if you just don't give up. No matter what you are trying to do or to accomplish, fulfillment of whatever it is that you want will require persistence on your part. If you don't persist, that dream will die. That thing that you want won't ever happen. If you give up prematurely, when things don't go or appear to go as planned, then you will miss out on what you could have accomplished or what you could have done. Allow yourself to personify persistence.

Persistence Personified

Michael Jordan once said, "I've missed more than 9,000 shots in my career. I've lost 300 games. 26 times I've been trusted to take the game winning shot and missed. I've failed over and over and over again in my life. And that is why I succeed."

Now, when you read that quote, it looks like failure. Then you might think, how can they say he's the best; how can they say that? Michael stated that he failed over, and over, and over again. But it doesn't end there, because his last statement that he made was powerful. He said, "And that is why I succeed."

All of the things that we do in life, those things that we keep trying to do, over and over, they may seem like they're not working. We are tweeting and trying to make things better.

What Michael was doing was perfecting his trade; he was perfecting his shots and his game in basketball. He was bringing all of those things together. Every shot that he missed caused him to be better. It caused him to focus more, to increase, and to be the best.

There is a phrase that I picked up a long time ago, that I even taught my kids, "Good, better, best, never let it rest, until your good is better, and your better is best." There are a lot of people we can look at in life who persisted beyond failures and achieved great success. That is exactly what Michael Jordan was implying in his quote. His failures made him better, and now he has gone down in history as being the best at his game.

We will all have to persist in order to get to that place that we want or envision. You may not be the best in your field or trade, but there is something that you are working toward. The point I'm making is that you must not give up. If you want something bad enough, you will have to keep working at it until you get what you want.

My next example is about one of my business mentors. He and his wife desired to purchase a $1.5 million dollar home that wasn't for sale. There was beautiful imported Italian marble in home, and his wife fell in love with the home when they toured it. She told him that she wanted the house, and he said, "Baby, if you want it, it's yours."

Then he called the realtor to put a bid on the home. The realtor called back to tell him that the home was not for sale and that it was only being used as a model home to sell the other homes. He and his wife then looked at other homes in the neighborhood, but they found nothing else that they liked. Their heart kept being drawn back to that model home that wasn't for sale. Most people would just give up when they had been told that the house was not for sale and was only being used as a model home. My mentor did not give up; he pursued his wife's dream home.

The first level of resistance appeared when the realtor told him that the house was not for sale. But he didn't let that stop him. He got creative. That's what you have to do when it's something that you want bad enough. You've got to get creative! My mentor then decided to call the company who owned the model home, and he asked why the home wasn't for sale. They told him that it wasn't for sale for two reasons: one, it was the model home that was being used to sell the other homes, and two, their sales offices were located in the basement of the home.

He was persistent again and created his own solution to the problem or obstacle that was before him. He asked them, "What if I purchased the home and allowed you to show the house on Sundays to help sell the other homes and allowed you to keep your offices in the basement for a year until you can build another home to show and relocate your offices?" He asked, "Would that work for you?" They said, "Sure, you've got a deal."

In spite of the obstacles he faced, he persisted. He and his wife purchased the beautiful dream home that they wanted! They were elated and happy. They got exactly what they wanted. My mentor was insistent with persistence that overcame resistance. We can all learn from this story. We must be insistent with persistence to overcome resistance that stands between us and our dreams.

Be insistent with persistence to overcome resistance.

My third example I found while researching a passion of mine. I am a seamstress from the heart. One of my passions is sewing. One of my desires that I haven't pursued at this point is to have my own fashion pattern line within one of the mainline home pattern companies such as McCall's or Simplicity. I did a little research about these companies and discovered an interesting story about a man who acquired McCall's Pattern Company and much more through the act of persistence.

My next persistence story is about Reginald Lewis, an American businessman. He was the richest African American man in the 1980s. Born in Baltimore, Maryland, he grew up in a middle-class neighborhood. He won a football scholarship to Virginia State College, graduating with a degree in political science in 1965. He graduated from Harvard Law School in 1968 and was a member of Kappa Alpha Psi. In 1992, Forbes listed Lewis among the 400 richest Americans, with a net worth estimated at $400 million. He also was the first African American to build a billion-dollar company, Beatrice Foods. After law school, Lewis started his own firm two years later. After fifteen years as a corporate lawyer with his own practice, Lewis moved to the other side of the table by creating TLC Group L.P., a venture capital firm, in 1983.

His first major deal was the purchase of the McCall Pattern Company, a home sewing pattern business, for $22.5 million. At the time, McCall's was number two in its industry, holding 29.7 percent of the market, compared to industry leader Simplicity Patterns with 39.4 percent. He managed to negotiate the price down and then raised $1 million himself from family and friends and borrowed the rest from institutional investors and investment banking firm, First Boston Corp. He got creative to attain funding for his business venture.

Likewise, if your dream or vision requires big capital, you've got to get creative in finding a funding source. There are so many options available now that weren't available when Mr.

Lewis started. People raise money online with help fund-me types of campaigns. You don't have to let the lack of money be a limitation to get started. Just take that leap of faith by doing something to get started and then ideas to attain the resources will follow.

Within one year, he turned the company around by making several strategic moves to strengthen McCall's by containing costs, improving quality, beginning to export to China, and emphasizing new product introductions. This new combination led to the company's most profitable year in its history. He later sold McCall's at a 90-1 return, resulting in a tremendous profit for him and for the investors. Those people who helped him initially as investors made millions of dollars. Lewis's share was 81.7 percent of the $90 million. The company's value grew from $26 million to $90 million. That was phenomenal results, but it did not end there!

In 1987, Lewis bought Beatrice International Foods from Beatrice Companies for $985 million, renaming it TLC Beatrice International, a snack food, beverage, and grocery store conglomerate that was the largest African American-owned and managed business in the U.S. Reginald Lewis used persistence to turn a possibility into an enormous probability of profit. We can take his story and ask ourselves, "What am I complaining about? What am I afraid of? What's stopping me from going after my dreams? Why do I allow anxiety or fear to hinder me?"

Oftentimes, we become anxious when things are not going our way or as planned, but we must learn to be persistent and overcome the obstacles. Anxiety wastes our energy. The image that comes to mind when I think of anxiety is like when you have one or more of the tires on your vehicle stuck in the mud. When you press down the gas pedal, hoping to pull yourself out of the mud, the tires just spin and splatter mud on everything. When it's all said and done, you are exhausted and someone else has to pull you out of the mud. Exhausting our energy on being anxious is wasteful. We need to preserve our energy to do those things that are productive and to do those things that will eventually yield desired results. Wasting present energy on a future undesired outcome is a muddy mistake. Don't spin your wheels, or waste your time thinking about something that you don't want to happen.

It drains our energy when our thoughts are consumed with the negative "what if" scenarios. The best way to control anxiety is to control our thoughts. Refocus your thoughts in your mind on the things that you desire and on the outcome that you desire to see, versus what you don't want to happen. That's exactly what these three men did. They didn't focus on the undesirable outcomes, but they focused their thoughts, their mind, and energy on the outcome they wanted to experience. And, guess what? They all succeeded.

What obstacle is before you right now that is discouraging you from moving forward to attain your dream or vision? What things are you feeling anxious about? If you are feeling overwhelmed or anxious, refer back to the Master Your Mindset chapter for techniques to help you get out of the mud.

My final example is from my own experience. As I stated earlier, I love to sew. At times, I also create patterns for clothing and home decor. When my twin sons were about six months old, I became a frustrated mom while transitioning them from solely breastfeeding to eating some solid baby foods. I was tired of ruining two outfits at the same time with orange carrot stains.

I wanted desperately to keep my babies' clothes clean from stains, so one early morning at my sewing machine, I was inspired with a witty idea to create a baby bib with zippered legs. I saw an image in my mind of what I should make. Then, I cut out and laminated the fabric and sewed two bibs with zippered legs. Then at our next mealtime, I put the bibs to the test. They protected my babies' cute clothes from becoming stained and I was a happy mom. Since I liked the results, I started sharing it and began to make them for other moms in the Mother of Multiples Group. They became my test cell group. As they provided input and suggestions. I tweaked my design. My test cell group helped me to perfect my design.

Then, I went on to apply for a design patent. Here is when I was faced with adversity and multiple obstacles. Instead of paying an attorney to do the patent application for me, I decided to save money and learn the patent process myself. It became a long-suffering process, but I grew in both knowledge and skills through it all. After mailing my patent application, the anthrax scare caused a federal mail lockdown. My patent application was stuck in mail for more than a year. Then finally, I received a letter stating that my application had been assigned for review. My application went through several revisions.

The most resistance that I met in the three-year process was when an examiner of my design at the Patent Office told me that my application would be rejected because my original sketch that I sent in with my application was different from the drawings submitted within my revisions. I almost wanted to give up, but I kept calling and kept making minor changes and resubmitting until my designs and application were accepted. Then my patent was granted.

And the sweet sign of victory was when I received my patent application and the official patent date was May 6, 2003. May 6th is my twins' birthday, and they were the inspiration for the Mr. Zippy Bib with Legs and Character. The Patent Office could have chosen any date of the year to grant my patent, but it was May 6th. That was a literal miracle. My persistence had paid off. I also took that date as a sign to continue to persist until something great happened with my bib invention. I went on to get a manufacturer, to get buyers, and the journey of persistence continues. I persisted to turn a pattern into a purpose.

It takes persistence to overcome resistance of any kind. In each of these stories, there were obstacles that each person had to navigate around. We all had to make adjustments to our plans, or had to face what we feared, and had to press through the resistance, which brought us closer to our dreams, closer to achieving our goal, and to the attainment of our hearts desire.

Persistence is the character trait required if the battle is long. If the path is not clear or straight, you must be consistently insistent with persistence to pursue your purpose. The purpose that I'm referring to is that thing or that goal that you are pursuing. The Apostle Paul wrote in Galatians 6:9 (KJV), "Let us not be weary in well doing: for in due season we shall reap, if we faint not."

Here's what to remember when you face obstacles:

1. Be persistent to overcome resistance.
2. Execute persistence to get assistance from a mentor to learn how they do what they do.

> It will cost you, but the monetary investments are worth it. You invest in yourself to get better and to benefit your desired outcome. I have personally invested thousands of dollars to become better. I've purchased coaching programs, audio training programs, and more, all to grow and to help grow my business. Now I'm offering the same help for others.

3. Your consistence in being persistent will help you go the distance. It may seem like a long stretch, but you can make it.
4. Become the resistance to obstacles that try to defeat the existence of your dreams.

Adversity Meets Persistence

Here's one more kind of weird story about being persistent in adversity. During one of my monthly Inside Out Empowerment Calls, a weird thing began to happen. Usually, on my conference calls, I can connect with my listening audience by phone and online. The online feature makes it easy for me to mute out all participants and then begin recording as I teach. Well, just as everyone was calling in, my internet went down.

At that time, I thought, "I can beat this; I'll just use another service that I have to record the call from my phone." I greeted everyone on the call from my phone and then asked them to hold while I started the recording. The recording started, but somehow it separated me from the listeners. I thought the call line was just muted, so I proceeded to teach. My topic was the "Power of Persistence."

When I reached the end of my teaching, I noticed that the recording had stopped, so I restarted it and was then instantly reconnected with everyone who was still patiently waiting for my return. I had no idea that I had been talking to myself for a whole hour. No one had heard a word that I had spoken. I've used my phone to record conference calls multiple times and that disconnect had never happen before. This was adversity in the weirdest kind of way. Two unrelated technical issues—how odd. My persistence was truly being tested.

I immediately called the participants who had been waiting on the conference line to apologize for the inconvenience and told them that I was persisting forward and would have another call on Thursday of that week. This became an "Adversity Meets Persistence" opportunity. I was determined to redo the entire teaching on the power of persistence because the adversity foreshadowed the blessing. The listeners were empowered to persist. We all learned the power of persistence from that experience.

CHAPTER 15: STEP OUT OF THE BOX

At one point in my life, I was seriously wanting to sell our home and buy another home with more space to accommodate our growing family. In addition to that, my heart had become discontented with the dated look of everything inside of our house, and I was frustrated that the exterior of our home was literally rotting away in some places. During that time, my older boys were just entering high school, and staying close to friends became their top priority, so getting a new house with more space was no longer a big deal to them. They even told me, "Mommy, you can get a new home after we graduate and go off to college."

Operating in the Faith Zone

With that said, I decided to snap myself out of feeling emotionally distressed about the size and condition of our home. I stopped looking for a new house and began looking for ways to give our house a new look. To start, I created a new Tote-a-Vision board that displayed what I wanted for our home. My thoughts elevated from a lowly distressed place to a higher place of discovery and possibility. I was now operating in the faith-zone again.

While keeping my thinking in the faith zone, I began to think outside of the box. The thought came to me, "You don't have to have money for everything you want. Why not use your skills in exchange for what you want?" Then, out of the blue, an old friend called to inquire about the steps to patent one of his ideas. Amazingly, that was my answer! Since he is an excellent carpenter, I was able to barter my *patent help 101* skills and services to get some of my desired home repairs done.

I did the legwork to complete my friend's utility patent application, and he provided his carpentry skills to do home repairs for me. He replaced all of the rotten wood on the exterior of our home. It was a great win-win. The home improvement project continued as we revamped the kitchen with updated cabinet fixtures, new appliances, and fresh paint throughout the house. The family room and dining room were given a facelift with new furniture, lighting fixtures, and accessories.

Since I love to sew, I decided to design and sew new curtains for each room in the house. For the boys' bedrooms I purchased new comforters, but I made dust ruffles and pillows to coordinate with the curtains. To free up more space in one of the bedrooms, I designed a bunk bed for my youngest son, then paid my carpenter friend to build it to fit above my oldest son's captain-style twin-sized bed. Once the frame of the bed was ready, my youngest son and I went to work on finishing it off with a beautiful golden oak stain and varnish that matched the captain-style bed. Then I bought new desks, chairs, and rugs to match the color themes. One bedroom had shades of red, chocolate, and beige, while the other had teal blue, crème, and chocolate. Lastly, to help pull in each of their interests, I found cool art to accessorize the rooms. When it was all said and done, my sons were super excited about their new personalized space. And it made me happy to see the smiles on their faces.

We literally had a new home within our existing home. My heart became happy and content again. As I took action by faith to work my plan, the right resources and opportunities showed up in a timely manner. I am always filled with gratitude when things just come together.

When you are feeling discontented or frustrated, the box that you are in may be too small. Your perspective about your situation may be limiting you. You may desire certain things to be different for your home and family too. What will it take to make your heart sing? Why not step out of the box and get in the faith zone to do something about it? Your opportunity awaits you.

CHAPTER 16: INFLUENCE YOUR DESTINY

Did you know that you have the power to influence your destiny? The outcome of your destiny depends on you. Your hopes and your dreams, your purpose or multi-purposes, are all intertwined within your destiny.

Say: I have the power to influence my destiny.

Say: I can be more, I can do more, I can have more.

In your notes, write the word Destiny. On the new few lines down, write the word Dreams on the left, then an equal sign (=), then on the right side write Desires.

A few more lines down write the word Dance directly under the word Destiny. Draw a vertical line down the center of Destiny and Dance. Draw a horizontal line under Dreams = Desires. Now you have a cross. In the center of the cross is a point of crossroads, a point of decisions.

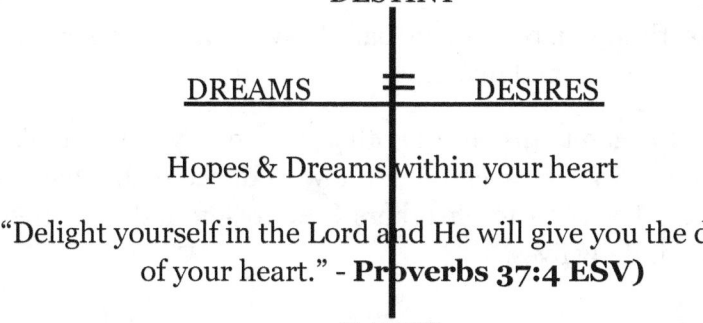

Hopes & Dreams within your heart

"Delight yourself in the Lord and He will give you the desires of your heart." - **Proverbs 37:4 ESV)**

You will have to use discretion to make the right decisions to get you where you want to be or go in life. Are you hoping to receive divine promises for your life? Delight yourself in the Lord and have discussions with your Divine Creator, and you will receive divine guidance. Those directions may come in night dreams or open visions. They may come through prophetic signs or by natural means. Whatever source they flow from, they are all intended to guide you.

Your destiny depends on how well you can dance. It will depend on how well you can dance with Divine in your life. Allow Him to lead and follow His lead or guidance and you will reach your Destiny.

As I mentioned earlier, during my college years I was introduced to the dance ministry. That is when the seed to dance as a form of worship was first planted inside of my heart. I began to discover a part of my purpose. For twenty years I taught others how to worship and praise through dance. I helped churches start dance ministries, taught at dance conferences, and even wrote a book about worship through movement. Out of obedience, I wrote down everything that I had learned about the dance ministry and worship. It was the dawn of a new day because I discovered more purpose. I discovered a love for writing. I discovered my potential to be a published author.

All these things happened in parallel with me being a wife, mother, engineer, and inventor.

In 2009, I began to discover another layer of my purpose. This new purpose was to teach others how to dance with Divine in their lives. I was to teach others how to let God lead them within their daily lives.

Dance with Divine

One of the major incentives that I hope you embrace from reading this book is to have a new awareness of your dance with Divine (God, your Divine Creator). Each chapter has provided instructions on how to get your life in focus to transform your dreams and goals into reality, and to ultimately influence your destiny. Your creator, God Himself, wants to provide guidance within each step of your journey to destiny. Remember this, when God is leading you, He is dancing with you. He is guiding you.

The more you trust God to order your footsteps and the more you obey in doing what He tells you to do, you are becoming a better dancer. I want you to understand that dancing with God is like ballroom dancing. Ballroom dancing requires the male to lead, and the female has to follow. When it comes to dancing with God, whether you are man or woman, you have to let God take the lead in your life decisions. As we allow God to take the male role, we, both men and women, are to submit and surrender to His guidance. God will order our steps to go in one direction, even when we think it is better to go in a different direction.

When I took ballroom dancing with my husband, it took some major adjusting for me. I had to learn how to relax and let him lead the steps in the dance. It was a challenge for both of us—I was a dancer from the heart, but dancing was not his thing.

As we journey, and we are working toward your vision, we are faced with many things. Here are some D's that you will face on your journey to Destiny.

D's in Your Destiny:

It all starts with your Dreams and Desires. You will have to use Discretion to make wise choices and Decisions. Make a decision to go after your dreams. You've got to make up your mind.

> *"Delight yourself in the Lord, and he will give you the desires of your heart."*
> **– Proverbs 37:4 (ESV)**

Discussions with God—pray—talk to God daily. Have a Daily Focus on your plans. Ask for insight on next steps. Have a discussion and ask for direction every single day.

Your Demeanor is very, very important. You've got to have a positive attitude about life. It doesn't matter what's going on, do your best to keep a positive outlook.

Develop a plan. Write down things that you can do. Create a to-do list.

Then, you must Do. Be a Doer. Be Dynamic by taking action. Having an action plan, but taking no action, results in dry bones and dead dreams.

During your journey to your Destiny, there will be a Discovery Process where you discover new things and acquire new knowledge and skills.

Dollars will be needed to fund your dreams.

Define your purpose within each phase or stage of your journey.

Be Diligent. Execute Discipline. Devote your time toward those things that matter.

Have Determination to keep going. Press your way through every challenge.

Digest new information. Take in new knowledge to grow. Allow yourself to stretch.

Keep a balance as you carry out your Duties. We all have different roles we play in our life, such as husband, wife, father, mother, employee, business owner, etc.

Make a Difference in the lives of others. You will see the Dawn of a New Day approaching, and remember to Dance. Dance with the Divine. Let God lead you in every step and through the process.

As you influence your destiny, you will be faced with challenges, but keep in focus that...

You can overcome:

Difficulties, Disappointments, Devastation, Detours, Delays, Distractions, and

Dry Seasons. Dry seasons are those periods when you are working your butt off, but nothing appears to be happening or changing for the better. Everything seems dormant.

At times, you will need to do Damage Control. When things go wrong or adversity interrupts your life, you have to drop everything and deal with it.

Sometimes, Depression might try to overtake you, but don't accept it as an option. You can think yourself into depression.

Be careful about being in Denial regarding areas where you need change, growth, or help.

Doubt cancels out faith, so it's not an option. Block out Doubt. Doubt is the biggest opponent to faith. They are in the boxing ring, duking it out. Believe in the possibilities and help faith win!

Disobedience to God delays our progress, so it's not an option. Be cautious of those times when you choose to do opposite of what you know in your heart is right.

Avoid things that drain or misuse your energy. Depleted energy is when you feel exhausted and you are too tired to work on your plan of action. If possible, avoid being around people who drain your energy over an extended amount of time.

Get your life in order to eliminate Disorganization.

Sometimes, we need Deliverance. We need healing from past hurts, hang-ups, fears, or past devastating experiences.

Have you ever tried something and you were knocked down and the experience scared you so bad that you wanted to give up? Those types of experiences can imprison you for years and hold you captive from living out your destiny if you do don't do something to break through to your deliverance.

As I shared earlier, when I was in high school, I had a very traumatic experience that caused a fear of speaking in front of people. That moment made an impression within my soul.

The fear of standing in front of people to speak became deeply rooted inside of me. It literally took me between ten to twelve years to break through that fear. After getting married, my husband had been taking some Dale Carnegie classes sponsored by his job. He suggested that I take the class. I agreed to take the class, but I was terrified to do some of the assignments. I would literally feel sick to my stomach and have to go to the bathroom before it was my turn to stand up. I recall one of the assignments was to recite a short quote several times in front of the class. That quote was, "To be enthusiastic, you must act enthusiastic!" Some people stood on top of the table and chairs, and they were expressive. The activity was meant to engage the audience, so people were laughing and cheering you on. To say the least, I did finish the class.

A few years later, a co-worker introduced me to Toastmasters International. It is a club that helps you develop your public speaking and leadership skills through practice and feedback. I made more progress while participating in that club, but what really helped me to break through the fear of speaking in front of people was after I accepted the call to minister. Having Bible studies in our home was cool, but when I had to start preparing sermons to minister each Sunday for church, it became a whole different ball game. My desire and passion to share a message that would change people's lives is what changed my life. For about two solid years, I forced myself to stand up each Sunday in front of the congregation. The repetition of standing up to deliver a message helped me to break through that fear.

Had I not followed through with taking the classes and doing the assignments, I wouldn't have received my breakthrough. Had I not followed through with joining the club, and practicing and receiving feedback, I wouldn't have my breakthrough. Had I not followed through with forcing myself to stand up to share a message before a small congregation of people every Sunday for almost two years, I wouldn't have my breakthrough. I definitely would not be traveling around the globe speaking in front of people to inspire them.

Do you need deliverance in an area of your life? Are you afraid to stand up in some area in your life because of a traumatic experience? If so, it's time to do something about it. It's time for your breakthrough!

Assignment:

Think back to an experience or to a time frame in your life where you became scared or became scarred deeply in your emotions. Once you pinpoint that experience, I want you to determine if it is still holding you back from becoming the person you know that you are supposed to be or if it is still holding you back from living out your dreams and goals.

Write down your experience or at least the emotion that is now holding you captive:

_____
_____
_____
_____
_____
_____
_____
_____

Next, write a statement to tell yourself that it will no longer hold you captive:

_____
_____
_____
_____
_____
_____
_____
_____

Next, get help! Speak with a counselor, hire a coach, take a class, etc. Write your next step:

_____
_____
_____
_____
_____
_____
_____
_____
_____

CHAPTER 17: JOURNAL TO SUCCESS

I will teach you some unique techniques that I have used for many years during my journaling journey. I will share how journaling brought insight, inspiration, and unfolded certain ingredients toward the success of reaching my goals.

As long as I can remember in my adult life, writing down my thoughts or taking notes have been a natural part of me, but for the longest time, I really didn't consider what I was writing as journaling. For one, I wasn't writing in a fancy leather-bound notebook like one would use for a diary. What comes to mind when you think of journaling? A big, leather-bound notebook full of long, handwritten notes? Deep, insightful reflections about your life, about society, human nature, or the soul? Famous diaries that later became books?

If these examples are what come to mind when you think of journaling, then, more than likely, keeping a journal is not at the top of your list, and you probably don't keep a journal. Or, if you have one, there is a high probability that you don't write in it regularly.

A lot of people claim that journaling isn't for them. But I think that resistance most often stems from a misunderstanding of what a journal can be. And those misunderstandings are usually based on what people have read or seen from outside sources instead of their own experiences. It's easy to opt out when we don't feel we measure up to an ideal—but in the case of journals, the ideal is totally fictional. People often assume a journal has a certain type of content. But the truth is, no two journals are alike, just like no two people who journal are alike.

A journal doesn't have to fit into a mold. It can be whatever you need it to be. There are thousands of different kinds of journals kept by millions of people all over the world. And I'd be willing to bet that, if you let go of your preconceived notion of what a journal *should* be and embrace whatever it is you *want* it to be, you'd find the practice of keeping one extremely rewarding.

While preparing to write this chapter, I decided to browse through several of my journal notebooks. Over the years, I have used composition-like notebooks and spiral notebooks as journals. I consider my journals as catch-all type journals, where about every aspect or focus in my life goes in them. My journals are extremely general and opened.

Write for Insight

As I browsed through my journals, I found what I've now identified as triggers that caused me to write. These same triggers may be helpful to you in getting pen to paper as well. Here are some of those triggers:

When you have thoughts about...

- New ideas
- Invention ideas
- Your vision, dreams, goals, and aspirations
- Your purpose and destiny
- Things that need to be done (that turn into a to do list journal entry)
- Significant events or experiences

Don't just think about these things. You should write it all down. Write it down and date it. The dates will help you chronicle your journal entries. Dates are numbers and they can be used to indicate the times and seasons in your life. Numbers can be symbolic or even prophetic in disclosing more insight to where you are in life.

For Example, on Sunday, July 17, 2016, the number 17 stood out for me.

1. I watched the *Joy* movie for the first time on July 17, 2016.
2. The book that Joy read to her daughter was about cicadas, which live underground and emerge after 17 years.
3. Based on a journal entry written in 1998, Moore of Rachel was incorporated in July 1998. At the same time, I incorporated "Signs & Wonders School of Creative Arts." The school never came into fruition and I dissolved that entity, but I think the name is significant and symbolic stating that MORI will become a sign and a wonder for me. In 2015, I launched the company MORI on September 9, 2015, which means for 17 years, the company had been in the background and now it has emerged like the cicadas. I had been doing business as my brand names, Mr. Zippy Bib, Mind Your Vision, and Tote-a-Vision, but not as Moore of Rachel Inc. (Note: Had I not made the journal entry, I would not have known the time and could have missed the significance of this season in my life.)
4. On July 31, 1998, written in my journal is a poem that I wrote called "The Fullness of Time." This poem was one page over from my journal entry about incorporating MORI, which was another sign that it was time to launch the company because the fullness of time had come to do so.

5. Seventeen years ago this year, I was inspired with the invention idea of the Mr. Zippy Coverall Bib.

6. My twin sons are 17 years old this year, and they inspired me to create the Zippy Bib.

7. May 6, 2017, will be another anniversary date for my first patent for the Mr. Zippy Coverall Bib.

8. Lastly, after journaling my thoughts about the *Joy* movie and all of the number seventeens, I read Esther chapter 7 where Esther makes her petitions and request to the king and the king granted her request. Guess which book of the Bible is Esther? Esther is the 17th book of the Bible.

Now, do you understand why you should write down the date whenever you make a journal entry? It can give you insight years later about where you are and about what you should be doing in your life.

Some other triggers that can prompt you to write:

- Night dreams
- Sermons
- Bible study
- Inspired thoughts or revelation
- Interesting people that you meet
- Thoughts about book titles or chapters that you want to write about

Reflect on the Information for Inspiration

Another journal entry that I found while preparing this lesson was made on May 10, 2004. At the top of the page is written

"And let us consider how we may spur one another on toward love and good deeds." – **Hebrews 10:24 (NIV)**

Right below the Scripture I wrote, "New Idea from God (A Motivation Course) - Create a course to teach others how to get out of a rut and to produce positive change in their lives. Re-teach the principles that I am learning, reading about, and applying to my life."

Next, I had a star next to the following words: "A part of my purpose is to motivate people to action— to positive change...To motivate people to not just settle for life as it is dealt out to them, but to take action to reach for more in life (1) how their household functions (2) finances (3) relationships (4) achieving goals (5) fulfilling dreams."

When I read this journal entry, I was astounded, because I'm living it right now. During that time of my life, my primary focus was the dance ministry and marriage ministry. I taught others how to worship through movement in dance and did a lot of couple's group sessions. Yet I was inspired with an idea to create a motivational course. Guess what? Unbeknown to me, that inspiration had become embedded in my mind, for eleven years later, that course was created. My Manifest More course was created in 2015 to motivate one to action to manifest more in their life. I can say that that idea has come to fruition.

Take time for Reflection

One of the best ways of developing a habit of reflection is through the practice of journaling. An experiment conducted and described in "Learning By Thinking" from Harvard Business School shows the importance of reflecting and learning from our experiences. The researchers put two groups of people through the same technical training. One group was asked to spend the last fifteen minutes of their day reflecting on what they had learned in a journal. The group that used the last fifteen minutes of the day to reflect in a journal, performed more than 20 percent better on their final assessment score than the group that did not. The bottom line is that learning happens when you make time to deliberately reflect on your experiences.

> *"We do not learn from experience, we learn from reflecting on experience."*
>
> – John Dewey, American philosopher, psychologist, and educational reformer

Those researchers also believe that self-efficacy was part of the reason for the better performance of the journaling group. Self-efficacy is defined as "the extent or strength of one's belief in one's own ability to complete tasks and reach goals."

It seems that the practice of journaling and reflection builds self-efficacy. That means if you want to grow your self-confidence, try combining reflecting on your experiences and journaling about those experiences. This happens because reflecting on your experience builds your confidence. It builds a strong belief in your skills and ability to achieve your goals. Write down your lessons learned about what went well, and what can be done better the next time to help improve your results. When you reflect on your action, you position yourself to perform better next time. It builds a belief and confidence in your ability to accomplish your goals. People who experience self-efficacy therefore invest more energy in their efforts, because they believe their efforts will result in success.

Gather the Ingredients

Learn to glean from the journal entries that you have made over the years. Key themes and ideas are the ingredients that you should combine together for a formula of success in your life. For example, if you wrote down lessons learned from an experience you had and then a month or two later, or even a year later, you wrote down lessons learned from another experience that you had, then you might combine those lessons learned into a book.

My journal entry on March 23, 2010, was written after quite time in a bubble bath. I wrote thoughts about the chapter layout of a book that I would one day write. I wrote down twenty chapters for the book and some content for the chapters. Six years later, I could use those chapters and content for a book. Had I not browsed and reflected on some of my journal entries, I would have never found this information.

Here are 10 ways you can use journaling to turn your goals into reality:

1. **Write it down:** Get it out of your head and onto paper. Share your heart. Write the vision and make it plain.
2. **Keep it focused:** Journal notes about your goals at least once a week. Not only will this keep your goals at the front of your mind, but each week you'll be reaffirming your commitment and the motivation behind wanting to achieve each goal.
3. **Visualize the outcome:** As you journal your desired outcomes, take a moment to visualize those outcomes. How are you going to feel about yourself when you reach a particular goal? How will your life be different? What other areas of your life will be positively affected by you reaching your goal?
4. **Track your progress:** Journal your milestones. When things in regard to your vision happen, write them down. You give yourself a progress report of what's going well, what you've found challenging, any obstacles that must be addressed or how you overcame

them. Also, journal what you've learned about yourself during the process. Knowledge is power, and this kind of progress review will help you stay on track. This is a good time to adjust your plans if necessary.

5. **Stay Accountable:** Journaling your goals and progress toward them reinforces accountability and is a reminder to commit to doing the next steps. At the end of each journal moment, ask yourself "Based on I just wrote, what actions I should take over the next week?"

6. **Give your inner affirming voice:** Writing is another avenue to voice what you feel in your heart. It's an avenue to express your thoughts and inner conversations about your desires. The Talk-Track that I shared with the Master Your Mindset Chapter is about your inner voice. Any goal worth achieving will be challenging, but you can write positive affirmations to keep your inner voice positive. Positive self-talk strengthens your willpower and self-compassion. When things get difficult, journaling is the perfect opportunity for giving your inner voice a positive perspective by practicing self-support through positive affirmations.

7. **Get creative:** Journal words, phrases, or quotes that empower you, then create inspirational art and frame it. Create a vision board with power words. Embrace new ways to motivate yourself to reach your goal.

8. **Explore your choices:** Reflect on past journal entries to see if there are any interesting patterns or observations, particularly in relation to the choices that you make.

Questions to ponder:
- Which goals am I not taking ownership and responsibility seriously?

- Which areas of my life am I avoiding because of unfinished business?
- Where am I saying, "I have to" instead of "I choose to"?
- Where am I giving my will power? Am I allowing others to dictate my decisions?

9. **Uncover self-limiting beliefs:** A huge part of attaining our desires or in reaching our goals is about personal awareness. Sometimes limiting beliefs that were established over time can hinder our growth and openness to new ideas. As you journal, look for evidence of any beliefs about yourself or things that might be holding you back. Then, ask yourself: Is there evidence that this belief isn't true? What actions can I take to let go of and overcome this belief?
10. **Give thanks and celebrate!** Every milestone counts as an opportunity to celebrate. As you journal, give thanks for divine guidance. Use your journaling to express your joy in achieving a goal and celebrate your wins. So often we forget to take a look back at the process we've made. Celebrate your progress by writing it down. You are creating a book of remembrance.

Different Types of Journals for Your Life Journey

Let's take a look at a few different types of journals you could keep to help give you insight and inspiration about your life. You don't have to have just one, blend different types together! It's your journey. Write what you want, when you want. That's what makes it your personal journal.

TOTE-A-VISION JOURNAL – GOAL JOURNAL

The Tote-a-Vision (TAV) Journal accompanies the Tote-a-Vision Board. You can track goals, ideas, milestones, achievements inside the journal. Write down names of people who can be instrumental to achieving your goal. List resources and resources that you might need. Use your TAV to capture photos, articles, new clippings, copied hand written notes from a different notebook, and any other item that can be used as a memorandum for the accomplishment of your vision, goals, and dreams. Your Tote-a-Vision becomes your personal inspirational guide to life.

CATCH-ALL JOURNAL

This is the type of journal that I use on a daily basis. It is a small spiral notebook that I carry with me everywhere I go. Whenever I have a thought that I want to capture, I write it down in my catch-all journal. My own journal is a mix of notes, lists, random thoughts, quotes, conversations, prayers, sermons, to-do lists, brainstorming notes, doodles, and "what I did today" entries.

NIGHT DREAM JOURNAL

If you have night dreams, record those that you can remember. Each morning before those fleeting thoughts and images about the dream disappear altogether, write them down. It's a good idea to keep your dream journal next to your bed. Write down the shell of what you can recall. Then record your thoughts or interpretations beneath the facts. Some dreams are prophet in proving you direction, insight, or warnings. Whether prophetic or not, it is a good idea to write them down to refer back to them later. Make it fun.

SCRIPTURE/PRAYER JOURNAL

Probably one of the most well-known types of journals, Scripture or prayer journals are a great way to dive deeper into your relationship with God. They can help you work through hard times in life as well as remember your blessings. You can examine your conscience, record your spiritual struggles, or just thank God for the happy moments. Writing down your prayers also enables you to recognize when you receive answers. Some people use this type of journal to help them study or memorize Scripture, too.

GRATITUDE JOURNAL

For some reason, it's always easier to turn to a journal when things are challenging. Adversity awakens a door to complaining or to discouraging thoughts. It can be a little depressing if all you have to look back on are pages filled with your struggles and complaints. A gratitude journal counteracts that negativity by helping you acknowledge the positives of daily life. Set a goal, and as regularly as works for you, write down a certain number of things you're grateful for. Record the small things that make you happy to the challenges that make you grow.

TRAVEL JOURNAL

When you travel, sometimes it's a challenge to set aside time to journal your new experiences. You don't want to miss capturing those moments, so at the end of each day during your trip, before retiring to bed, take a few moments to write down what happened today. Include what you saw, people you met, places you visited, and who spent that time with you.

PHOTO JOURNAL

The smart devices that we carry around with us all have built-in cameras, which make taking photos easy. Why not create a photo journal? On the pages of your photo journal, add comments you want in the margins next to each photo. It's sort of like scrapbooking or creating a photo album, but with a slight twist.

PROJECT JOURNAL

With this type of journal, you keep track of your actions and progress on any project of your choosing. It's a good way to stay accountable, to evaluate the success and a place to note barriers that should be addressed. Write down your successes as well as lessons learned from different actions taken throughout the project. Write down your overall action plan. Note the overall status of your project and what next steps you want accomplished. Refer back to your journal regularly and use it to help you keep moving toward your end goal.

BUCKET LIST JOURNAL

If you have a mental bucket list, why not write those thoughts down and create a bucket list journal? Journal when, where, and how each experience unfolded. Then cross the item off the list. Place your list at the front of the journal, and leave room for future additions. Make an entry each time you achieve one of your dreams from your list. You can choose to make your entries short or long, just be sure to include details that you want to remember many years later. Also record your thoughts about that experience.

How to Get Started

Start with making a journal entry at the end each day. Set a goal to end each day reflecting on the events of your day.

Here are some ideas to help you get started:

1. **To Get Started, Ask Yourself some Focused Questions.**

    As you go through each question, reflect on the experiences, thoughts, and feelings that occurred.

    - What things did I accomplish that were on my to-do list?

- What things did I accomplish that were not on my to-do-list for today, but are a step toward reaching my goal?
- What are the things I consider important work, and did I do that today?
- How did I maximize my time? Did I use my time wisely?
- How much time did I waste? What didn't work today?
- Did I learn anything new or gain new insight?
- What's next? What should I focus on tomorrow? What are three important tasks I want to accomplish tomorrow? (This last question is to help you create a To-Do list for tomorrow.)

Use the questions to guide you in writing your journal entry. Write in your journal about what you did during the day, how you felt, where you failed, and what you didn't get done. The idea is to write thoughts about your day. Explore what you did, where you *fail short*, and how you felt about the experiences.

2. **Avoid too Much Structure**
Keep your journaling fairly simple and unstructured. Too much structure could halter the flow of thoughts. It could also hinder your motivation to write. There is no one right way to journal, just practice to find what works for you. Feel free to adjust your journaling process to your liking. The most important thing is that you get into the habit of reflecting on your day and write about it.

3. **Look for Ways to Improve**
Once you have gotten into a habit of journaling, after a few months, take time to read through your entries. As you read, look for patterns. Are there recurring themes,

thoughts, emotions, or habits? Is there anything that you can learn from these patterns? What can you change to become more effective?

Journaling is a really good personal development tool that will help you learn, grow and improve. Ultimately, it can help you be more, do more, and have more in all areas of your life.

Start Your Journey Now

Do not wait. If something is holding you back, now is the time to let go of what you cannot control. The only person you can change is yourself. Focus on what you have control over. Get excited about your future, because the future is indeed bright for you. As you transform your dreams and goals into reality, you are being transformed from the inside out. Your life is going to improve as you *mind your vision*. Get ready to experience extraordinary results!

Napoleon Hill, author of *Think and Grow Rich*, said, "Do not wait; the time will never be 'just right.' Start where you stand, and work with whatever tools you may have at your command, and better tools will be found as you go along."

The next section will walk you through mindful methods to get "IT" to flow. The IT in each step represents what you want to create in your life. You are transforming from the inside out. Your life is going to improve as you *mind your vision*.

Chapter 18: Apply Mindful Methods

Mindful Methods

Before you start this section, download the free workbook. The *Working IT Out* workbook is the Application Section which accompanies each step in the Mindful Methods portion of this book. You can download the workbook at https://mindyourvision.com/workbook/

The first step is how to recognize your "IT." IT represents what you want to create in your life. To recognize IT, you need to get connected and get in the flow. Learn how to listen to that inner voice that desires to guide you and respond immediately.

God will drop thoughts in your mind and desires in your spirit. Then your heart will start pulling you toward IT. That IT is whatever that desire is that's in your heart that you begin to give attention to. Don't worry about the HOW. Trust the process and provision will come in the right time.

Get IT to Out

Step 1: Get IT out

Now that you've recognized what IT is for you, the next step is to get that desire out of your heart or head by putting IT in written and then in visual form. Create a vision board that represents your vision. Keeping a visual reminder will take your written vision to a whole new level.

I encourage you to complete Step 1 with a friend, family member, colleague, or business partner. Studies show that you are more likely to reach a goal if you have a partner. The reason this works is that you can hold each other accountable.

With family visioning, you teach your children how to believe in their dreams too. They will gain firsthand experience in creative goal setting. As your children learn to tap into their God-given abilities, they will begin to see things happen based on their beliefs and actions. That is exactly what happened with my sons, as I shared earlier in the book. My sons have continued to succeed year after year. They now understand the power of faith, visualization, and self-empowerment.

Five Tote-a-Vision Steps for Obtaining Your IT

- Think IT – Take the time to decide what you want. Imagine the possibilities. Do not limit yourself based on your present circumstances.
- Write IT – Utilize the workbook to write down your desires.
- Picture IT – Search for images, pictures, and power words that reflect your desires, like being debt-free, more family time, travel, etc. Cut and paste those items onto the white board provided with your Tote-a-Vision.
- Tote IT - Insert your completed vision board into the large vinyl pocket of the Tote-a-Vision sleeve. It will provide both protection and visibility for your visual masterpiece. Wrap the vinyl sleeve around a composition size journal. You are ready to tote your vision everywhere you go. If you decide to keep it flat, your Tote-a-Vision can be displayed on a refrigerator, desk, or wall. It will be there in times of triumph or in times of discouragement to keep you focused on your goals.

- Track IT - Utilize a journal to track your results, your ideas, and your milestones.

Now that you've got IT out and onto your board, it's time to get IT to flow in your life. That means you have to get in the flow.

It requires focus to get in the flow! Over the next thirty, sixty, or ninety days, it's your choice to decide the length of this challenge. I encourage you to focus your attention, your daily intentions, and your time and energy toward specific goals that catapult you toward your vision. You will utilize the power of the present (now), imagination, visualization, intuition, applied faith, persistence, determination, and focus to accomplishing your goals.

Step 2: Get IT to Flow

We will cover several stages in the Get It to Flow step. Remember your IT is whatever you want it to be in your life. These stages will guide you to unblock IT, unlock IT, visualize IT, affirm IT, believe IT, attract IT, recognize IT, receive IT, use IT, and give IT.

Unblock IT

To get things flowing in your life, you must unblock wasteful thoughts or beliefs. Make an assessment.

Ask yourself the following questions:

- What am I doing that hinders my flow or would hinder me from receiving what I desire?
- What type of thoughts about myself do I entertain daily?
- What beliefs do I have that are contrary to what I desire to attain?

Unblock the limitations, which include:

- Negative thinking
- Disbelief and doubt
- Focusing on current circumstances
- Not seeing the forest for the trees
- Listening to people with negative words and attitudes
- Fear—fear of failure, fear of the unknown, fear of others' opinions
- Past negative experiences
- Mental conditioning—you were taught to think or believe a certain way
- Procrastination – avoiding a task that would move you closer to your dreams
- Complaining or blaming versus taking personal responsibility for your circumstances

> *Don't allow yesterday's messes to spill over into today's successes.*
> *– Rachel Moore*

Unlock IT

After you identify the blockages, the next step is to release the old thought patterns, self-limiting beliefs, and habits. Replace them with thoughts and actions that reflect your desired results. Unlock your potential to imagine bigger things!

Begin speaking what you want in the present tense. Through your clear declaration, you can control your inner voice. Be more encouraging and affirming.

Words and Works

Words are powerful. Words are seeds. What you plant will bear fruit. Whether positive or negative, words planted will take root, grow, and bear fruit that reflects its kind. To move in your desired direction, all your words must be in alignment.

- Spoken words
- Words in thought
- Written words
- Words in action (our work)

The words we speak, think, write, and act upon, must all align and agree with our desires. Your thoughts are the primary driver for written and spoken words.

As you analyze your thoughts and feelings, consider how words take form. Your thoughts are words, but you also verbalize words and write words. To move in your desired direction in life, all your "words" must be in alignment. For instance, if you want to turn one of your hobbies into a business, you might first write down your idea. Then you might think about all the possibilities that your business can provide for you and your family. You share the idea with your family and even purchase items to get started. But if you never act on working your business, it will not develop. Therefore, the words that you speak, think, write, and act upon must all align with your desires.

Visualize IT

Visualize your desires. This starts with creating a vision of what you want in your mind's eye. My acronym for VISION is **V**ibrant **I**mages **S**ignifying **I**deal **O**pportunities **N**ow. Visualization requires both concentration and imagination. Find vibrant images that reflect your desires, and then visualize your desired outcome. There is always something that you can be doing to work toward your goals right now. Look for opportunities and expect new ones to unfold in your life.

We have all heard, "A picture is worth a thousand words." Rather than just saying what you want in words, why not say it with pictures? Picture your dreams and goals. Our minds respond to images and pictures. Our minds begin to believe what we envision. Once we believe that something is possible, we can achieve it. You can support your imagination with a visual aid such as a vision board.

> *"Imagination grows by exercise, and contrary to common belief, is more powerful in the mature than in the young."*
> — Paul McCartney

I have learned that you must act immediately on ideas or hunches that you divinely receive. You are being guided to the next step in your journey, which will get you closer to attaining your goals, big or small.

Use your imagination, the creative faculty of your mind, to visualize your desires as if they were true right now. You may ask why visualization is so important. Our minds retain pictures or images more readily than written or spoken words. Pictures stimulate and increase desire. That is why television advertisement works so well. Most of all, pictures can enhance your capacity to believe what once seemed impossible to achieve.

Various techniques have been tested to strengthen our ability to visualize. One of the more popular and proven techniques is to create a vision board. A vision board can also be referred to as a dream board, focus board, or life map.

Affirm IT

Take action daily and begin speaking what you want in the present tense. Affirm your desires and goals by bringing your thoughts, words, and action into alignment.

Believe IT

To believe is to accept as true. It requires a lot of emotional energy to believe, especially when there are others around you speaking words of doubt that bring discouragement.

> *"Whatever the mind can conceive and believe, it can achieve."*
> – Napoleon Hill

Attract IT

We are surrounded by spiritual laws, scientific laws, governmental laws, and universal laws. The law of gravity is a scientific law that can easily be tested. Just take an object and drop it. What happens? It falls to the ground. If we choose to work against gravity, we will suffer the consequences. Understanding aerodynamics allowed man to create airplanes and rocket ships that supersede the law of gravity.

Applied faith attracts your IT into your life. The principle of faith operates within spiritual laws. Since faith is a principle, it must be put into practical use to get results. Applied faith makes you a magnet. As your mind believes, faith attracts your desires in the physical realm. What you desire is what you hope for and want to manifest in your life. Your goals are presently unseen in the physical realm, but they can be real within the mind's eye.

As you unlock your mind to believe, you will release faith that operates within the spiritual realm. Every image and word that you have placed on your Tote-a-Vision board is a visual picture of what you are hoping to become a reality. As you exercise your faith, you will begin to see your desires manifest.

You put your faith to the test by writing down your desires, creating a visual reminder, and taking daily action toward your goals. So do what it takes to believe and *block doubt out!*

Doubt causes the cord of faith to shred and hinders the attraction process.

Ideas, opportunities, people, and resources will appear almost out of the blue to aid in your quest. As you continue, you may or may not notice that some things are already set in motion because of your strong desire and belief. Things will manifest if you keep believing and seeking inspiration.

As I've stated before, faith works in conjunction with spiritual laws to form manifestations in the physical realm. Faith takes on the form of whatever you believe. Do not worry about how faith will form what you desire. Your job is to believe and not doubt. You must focus your thoughts on what you want, visualize with your mind's eye, and accept it as if you already possess it. Then, ultimately, what you hoped for will become a reality.

Another spiritual law to be aware of is the law of sowing and reaping. Whenever we sow seeds of thoughts, words, or actions, we will eventually reap fruit accordingly. Therefore, pay attention to what you are sowing. Begin with the end in mind. Decide what you want to reap, and then begin sowing the proper thoughts, words, and actions for your desired harvest.

Apply faith to belief by having a positive mindset, a clear vision, and appropriate actions. Spiritual laws will work in your favor. You must act as if IT is already yours. We must "be" before we "become." "To be" is dynamic. We must act so that our desires become a reality.

"Life is too short to waste. Dreams are fulfilled only through action, not through endless planning to take action."
–David J. Schwartz

Recognize IT

New ideas will come to mind, assignments will present themselves, and people and resources will be provided as aid to you on your journey to reach your goals. It is up to you to recognize what is being provided. To receive, you must first recognize the provision. Expand your mind. Do not worry about the "how" now, just be open to recognize and receive the "how" when it comes.

After you recognize your provision, you must take the next step. Action will always be a requirement. Without work, faith is dead. Your IT will not manifest without work.

Receive IT

Now it is time for your reward. All you have to do is receive as your desires manifest into the physical realm.

Use IT

You will experience various phases of growth during your transformation journey. Use the knowledge you are gaining and the understanding you are cultivating. If you do not apply what you are absorbing, it is useless. *Use it or lose it.* Enjoy what you have. Whether it is new knowledge, new skills, or new wealth, use it for good.

Give IT

The law of increase operates through giving and service. If you desire a continuous flow of abundance in your life, align yourself with a purpose for the greater good.

Step 3: Get the Future in the Now – "Act As If"

Acting as if requires out-of-the-box thinking, doing things outside your comfort zone, and speaking everything in the present tense. Live life and do things as if you already have what you want.

One of my most creative *act as if* moments was a few years ago following my husband's first extended job loss. At the time, he had been out of work for quite some time. Applying for jobs online became routine. The application process and the responses became all too familiar.

One day after work, an idea popped in my head. I decided to give my husband a surprise party to celebrate his job-to-be. He had applied for two jobs online the night before, so I thought, "Why not celebrate as if he already has the job?"

I phoned my sons to tell them we were having a party to celebrate their father's job-to-be and that I would bring home pizza for dinner. Although they did not quite understand, they were excited. I stopped by a store to pick up a card, balloons, and table decorations.

My husband was out when I arrived home, which gave me time to prepare the house for our celebration. When he returned home, the kids and I yelled, "Congratulations!" Startled, he asked, "Congratulations for what?" We told him that we were celebrating his job-to-be. We all enjoyed the meal and time together as a family that evening. In only a few days following our *act as if* new job celebration, my husband received a phone call for an interview. And what was even more amazing, within ten days, he had started his new job.

One of my more recent "Act as If" experiences occurred while training to compete in an all-natural bodybuilding competition. For many years I have practiced having a healthy, fit body through moderate exercise. However, even though I am petite with a small frame, I still had belly fat issues. A couple of friends who are professional bodybuilders challenged me to compete. I hired them to train me. That challenge pushed me beyond limits in my body where I discovered new strengths and potential.

During the training period, I worked my butt off to prepare for the stage. Each morning I had to push and encourage myself with positive affirmations, scriptures, and prayer. I told myself, "You can do this. You are a winner!"

As my trainers coached me, I modified my diet and started doing daily meal preps. Acting as if I were a pro at body building, I increased the frequency and lengths of my cardio and weight training. I even hired a posing coach to train me in posing in a bikini. Since I'd never worn a bikini in my adulthood, posing in a bikini was definitely out of my comfort zone.

For two months straight, I had to engage my mind to think and to act like a pro. I adjusted my schedule to fit in more exercise, more water intake, and more sleep to prepare my body. I competed in two categories: Open Bikini and Bikini Masters. It was show time! While on stage, I had to *Act as If* I was a pro. I had to walk with confidence and grace in 4.5" heels while being judged by a panel of professional body builders. They looked at every muscle and at every pose. In addition to all of that, I had to remember to keep a smile on my face throughout the entire time I was being judged.

It all paid off! Surprisingly, I placed 4th in the Open Bikini, where I competed against ladies who were in their twenties and thirties. Having recently turned 50, I was the most mature lady on stage in that category. In the Bikini Masters category of ages 40 and older, I won 1st place. My vision for a lean tummy was surpassed with a vision to win, and it all manifested. It was my first-time competing in this nature, but I took home two trophies! My family was there to celebrate the big win. My three sons in college even came home to support me at the show. We took lots of photos. They even captured the moment of me eating a donut. It was delicious! After the show, the Competition Host had passed out donuts to all of the contestants to enjoy.

That experience taught me a few things. First of all, I grew to respect bodybuilding as a true sport. It takes a lot of self-discipline and perseverance to prepare your body to compete on stage. Next, I learned that you must push through to overcome the battles in your mind, because your thoughts can either cripple you from starting, or they can push you to finish with a trophy-sized win. It all starts in the mind. Lastly, it taught me a whole new way of living. I now do a lot of weekly meal preps to control what I eat, but not as strict, of course. Following the competition, I adjusted my lifestyle to low-carb living and still do moderate exercises weekly.

While preparing my body for the stage, I surpassed the fitness goal to trim my tummy and firm up my abs. It was an extremely challenging journey. However, through faith, focus, determination, and a lot of working out, and following strict meal plans, I not only achieved my goal, but discovered new potential.

You can get your future in the now through actions and through affirmations. Affirmations will help you view life through a different set of lenses. You will begin to see through your minds-eye vision instead of focusing on what you see happening with your physical eyes. You start to integrate your desires into your belief system as you speak the affirmations as if they were already true in your reality. One of the things that I do to strengthen my belief is to speak aloud Scriptures. It makes my statements even more powerful to agree with an established truth.

Now it's your turn. If you haven't already done so, go ahead and start writing down a few statements that you want to become your reality. Even look up a few Scriptures that support your cause and add them to your list of affirming statements. Contrary to your belief about your current circumstances right now, begin to speak aloud your written affirmations. Speaking those things that are not yet real as though they were is an act of faith. Over time, as you do this, your state of mind will be transformed into a new way of thinking. Your conversations will be different. Even your view of life will become a bit more optimistic.

An abbreviated version of a famous quote sums up what this book is all about. I've added my spin on it by inserting the word "belief" between the "words" and "actions." And, so it says the following:

> *"Watch your thoughts, for they become words.*
> *Watch your words, for they become beliefs.*
> *Watch your beliefs, for they become your actions.*
> *Watch your actions, for they become habits.*
> *Watch your habits, for they become character.*
> *Watch your character, for it becomes your destiny."*

In retrospect, you have the power to influence your destiny.

Start your journey now. Do not wait. Let go of things that no longer serve you. If there is something that is holding you back, now is the time to let go of what you cannot control. The only person you can change in life is yourself. Focus on what you have control over. Get excited about your future, because the future is indeed bright for you. You are transforming from the inside out. Your life is going to improve as you mind your vision.

It starts with a feeling on the inside of you that there is more to life for you than the present. If you embrace the thought, then God will start to grow that desire in you. You can embrace the next larger part of yourself. It's new potential and new possibilities being discovered.

CHAPTER 19: BE INSPIRED TO ASPIRE

Hopefully by now after reading about some of my personal experiences and victories, you are already inspired to aspire further by going after your hopes and dreams. However, if you need a little more push, here are stories about others who reached or surpassed their goals. Here's how Tote-A-Vision is working for kids of all ages.

You teach your children how to believe and how to tap into their God-given abilities, and they will begin to see things happen for them outside of your control. That's exactly what happened with my sons.

Family visioning with Tote-a-Vision keeps your children motivated. They see where you are going as a family. It keeps everyone on the same page. You put a picture on your faith and help them to see more and to achieve more. It's working for my family.

When used in schools, it has worked in classrooms as well. I received a letter from one teacher who worked at an alternative school, where the trend is that some students keep repeating—they leave, and they are sent back to the alternative school. She invited me into the classroom, and I introduced the Tote-a-Vision. She started using it with her students. The results have been astonishing because most of those students are no longer returning.

So when a new student comes through, she makes sure that she takes them through the visualization and dreaming process, and they create their Tote-a-Vision. One of the things that we noticed is that these kids have big dreams in their hearts. They don't really tell anybody, or if they did, someone might shoot it down because of the environment that they are growing up in. When I went around the classroom, some of those students wanted to be doctors, lawyers, actresses, and professional athletes. They all had huge, huge dreams, and I told them, "Do you realize that the path that you are on will not get you to that dream? You've got to be on a different path, so use your vision board to remind you of where you want to be." After they received the right tools, guidance and direction, they began to see, and it motivated them to change their behavior. Use the vision board to get them thinking. Get them wanting it bad enough and they will change their own attitudes and actions.

The YMCA in Ohio partnered with me to implement one of their student programs. They are using the Tote-a-Vision (TAV) with 250 students in two different areas. To accompany their TAV, I prepared special materials to guide them through a goal-setting process. The organization used it to help students create goals on how they will attain enough credits to graduate. They also used it with the more advanced students to teach them higher levels of goal setting.

A single entrepreneur mom brought her 10-year-old son to one of my weekend seminars. He created his Tote-a-Vision and shared with us what he wanted. He wanted to attend one the most exclusive and expensive private schools in the county. He wanted to learn how to scuba dive and he had several toys that he wanted. About four months later in a meeting with this mom, she tells me, "Rachel, you won't believe it. Just about everything on my son's vision board has happened. Out of nowhere, he receives a paid in full scholarship to attend that private school. Then I received in my email a coupon for a scuba diving lessons at a great price."

The same mind-freeing techniques and faith-building concepts taught throughout this book, also works for financial increase. One real estate investor shared with me what happened after going through the Tote-a-Vision Financial Freedom workbook in conjunction with her vision board. She began thinking differently and was no longer boxed in by old limiting-beliefs. She had several properties that she wanted rented. Within one month of visualizing and going through the workbook, every property was rented. She had met a person at a networking meeting who was associated with placing military families. Her properties were listed as a housing resource, and every vacancy was instantly filled.

You can apply this to your health, to your wealth, and to your relationships. A young lady in one of my workshops created a relationship Tote-a-Vision board. She began to practice the techniques, and within six months, she went from zero to hero. She met her soul mate and is now engaged.

A few years ago, a more mature woman, who was divorced and praying for a new love, attended one of my small group sessions. During our "Create your Tote-a-Vision" session, she found images and words to reflect exactly what she wanted to experience in her life. She is now remarried and living her dream life. Her business expanded, and she and her husband recently purchased their dream home together. (Photo previous page.)

VIEW VISION BOARD EXAMPLES at
https://mindyourvision.com/gallery/

Chapter 20: Be Smart With Your Goals

This final chapter is like your check and balance sheet. You can use it to determine if you are on track with reaching your goals. Let's talk about SMART goals. The original acronym for SMART first appeared in the November 1981 issue of *Management Review*. "There's a S.M.A.R.T. way to write management goals and objectives" was the title, and it was written by George Doran, Arthur Miller, and James Cunningham.

On the following page, see the SMART acronym with my modified version of definitions. Goals. First of all, we want to be smart with our goals. Since I have already covered most of the points in detail throughout this book, we will mainly focus on the M and R portions of SMART that relates to *measuring* and *recording* results. I added the BE because reaching our goals starts with our BEHAVIOR. How we behave in our mind and in our actions determine what we will have or receive. Read over each part of BE SMART, and then we will review M and R in detail.

BE SMART with Your Goals

B – Believe (and not doubt), Burning desire and Block doubt

E - Energy - Energize your mind, will, and emotions. Encourage yourself to stir up enough passion to motivate you to go after your dreams and goals.

S - Set Specific Goals. (See it, Speak it, Script it) Write out your goals.

M - Mind Your Vision. (Use your mind to create a mental image of your desires; use your mind to picture what you want in your minds-eye.) Measure your progress (put measures in place to help you stay on track).

A - Attitude, Affirm, Action. (Have a positive attitude (think positive), affirm your goals with present tense affirmation statements, and then take massive action towards your dreams and goals. Write and speak words and statements that affirm your desires in the presence tense.

R - Reflect, Record, Refine goals, Revisit, Resources (use them), Results, (write down your goals, your ideas, your results, and milestones).

T - Thankful - be grateful for what you have, thankful for the process; be thankful for the small and the big. Test the waters—don't be afraid to test and try the ideas and opportunities that come to you or along your way.

Once you have established your list of goals on paper and/or on your vision- goal board, the next step is to develop an action plan or action steps. Once you execute those action steps, how will you determine if you are making progress? What kind of measures can you put in place to help you stay on track?

Measures must be relevant to your goals. If your goal is to save X amount of dollars for a dream vacation, you wouldn't use the number of social media posts as a measure for that goal. Instead, you would use the frequency of deposits or the amounts deposited in some frequency as a measure. You might list the different sources that are providing income toward the savings. The measures set to track your results toward project goals at work would be totally different. So as you establish your goals, it's important to think through ways to measure your progress toward your desired results. Revisit your measures often enough and make adjustments as needed. Sometimes you may need additional resources to help you reach your goal. For example, to complete this book, I hired additional resources help with the editing, formatting and design.

The R is for recording your results, for reflecting on the process or progress that you are making and then refining your plan to better hit your targets. I personally use the "R" points often when I record my results as journal entries. My journaling entries and notes provided content for this book. The stories that I shared about my family came directly from my journal notes and place where I had recorded the story.

Challenge yourself to BE SMART with your goals. As we conclude, there is a brief recap of the Mind Your Vision System.

TESTIMONIALS FROM INDIVIDUALS WHO ATTENDED *MIND YOUR VISION* SEMINARS:

I just wanted to let you know how inspiring and informative your presentation was during Wednesday night services at Harvest Cathedral. I've never heard you speak publicly, but you are a fireball and I hung on to your every word. The information you presented about the vision board was very clear and well planned. You are very well spoken and articulate.

I have shared with many of my friends about the vision board and I can't wait to get some copies of the DVD to distribute.

– Wendy Williams

*****

The seminar gave me practical steps to make my dreams come true. I gained a sense of the importance of being positive at all times. The vision board made me excited about my dreams. I enjoyed the stories that were shared and would like to hear more about successful individuals who changed their lives through vision and positive attitude.

– Lisa

*****

"As an entrepreneur, I face daily challenges in growing my business; the biggest challenge all entrepreneurs face is doubt, fear, and discouragement. The Tote-a-Vision that I carry with me daily provides me with a physical reminder of most significant WHYs in my life. The Tote-a-Vision Financial Freedom workbook combined with the Tote-a-Vision helps me stay focused on achieving my life vision; it's a complete system that anyone with a dream needs to succeed."

– Diane W., entrepreneur, The Deal Fairy

*****

The seminar exceeded my expectations. The knowledge on how to make a dream board was powerful. I will create my first dream board specifically for my goal to complete college.

– J. Thorpe

*****

The seminar most definitely met and exceeded my expectations. The presentation gave me ideas I can use with my child. I like to write and journal. I learned how to continue to encourage and inspire my child to meet the goals and dreams of her future.

– Ann M.

*****

Yes, the seminar met my expectations. It definitely presented practical and affordable information. I gained so much for understanding the "power words" and dream board. Learning the use of it and the importance of discussions at home about our hopes and dreams was also valuable.

– Anonymous

*****

The seminar did meet my expectations. The idea that we see in images in our minds rather than in words was a light bulb moment for me. Personally, I will create a dream board for my new home and yard. And for my family, I will create one with my goals for my children.

– Kathryn Short

*****

The seminar was very informative, encouraging, and inspiring. I will create a dream board for my family and definitely use what I've learned to inspire my grandchildren.

– Anonymous

*****

The seminar met my expectations. It was very inspiring. I also learned creative ideas that will inspire my children to help build their self-esteem.

– Susan Daniels

*****

This seminar absolutely exceeded my expectations. What I gained most from the seminar was learning about the necessary tools to encourage and cultivate my dreams as well as my children's dreams and goals. I am so excited about getting started with my vision board.

– Christine Cruse

*****

The seminar went above and beyond my expectations. I learned more ideas on how I can accomplish my goals and dreams. I look forward to creating my vision boards specifically for my family and finances.

– D. Goolsby

*****

Since attending the "Power Up Your Dreams" seminar hosted by Mind Your Vision, where I created my relationship vision board, I have met so many men. My girlfriends are laughing at me, going from zero to so many options in such a short period of time. I'm amazed at the results that I'm getting in my life.

– Felicia G.

*****

My response to Felicia:

See what happens when you focus your heart and intentions on a specific area in your life. You put your mind and heart on finding the right pictures, images, or words for your relationship vision board. Little did you know that action of faith would move God to respond to your request so quickly—from zero to several options. That's amazing!!!

The vision board is like writing your vision, only it is in a visual form. We are operating in an act of obedience and that pleases God. We are also activating our faith, which also pleases God and causes Him to move on our behalf.

Now is a good time to create your personal vision board. If you already have one, what next steps are you taking toward the fulfillment of your dreams?

CONCLUSION

In the heart and mind is where the conception of a dream begins. From conception, that dream must be nurtured by a positive mental and emotional environment. It requires focus, determination, and perseverance. Excuses and doubt can completely abort our dreams. But when you believe, anything can happen! Napoleon Hill, the author of *Think and Grow Rich*, said it best, "Whatever the mind can conceive and believe it can achieve."

Once you give yourself permission and make a decision, then things will start happening for you. I want you to start living your dreams, fulfilling your desires, and moving forward into your greatness. Ask yourself, what is it that I want? Once you know what you want, you can begin making progress. In life you have either excuses or results, but you can't have both. It has been said that 99% of failure comes from people making excuses.

Let's recap the Mind Your Vision System that you can follow to achieve your hopes and dreams.

1. **Vision:** It all starts with a dream, a passion, a desire that you can visualize.

2. **Believe:** You must believe in yourself and believe in your dreams. What do you believe you can do?

3. **Cancel Doubt Out:** In order to do or to achieve anything you want in life, you must change your

mindset. Instead of saying you can't, say, "I can." Pay attention to what you allow into your mind. If your mind is filled with negative thoughts, then there's no room for new ideas. Change your thinking process.

4. **Make a Decision:** Decide what you want. Stop making excuses, and make a decision about something in whatever area in your life you want to change.

5. **Clarity of Vision:** Write down your hopes and dreams. Get them out of your head and heart onto paper. Then map them out with images.

6. **Action:** Belief without action results in dead dreams. There are many dreams that go to the grave because people were afraid to take action.

7. **Total Commitment:** Be totally committed to your dreams and to your passion. Have a stick to it attitude until you reap results. Ninety-nine and a half percent won't do.

8. **Accountability:** Hold yourself accountable for the results that you want and for whatever you're doing. When you remove yourself from the accountability formula and place blame on someone else for things not happening the way you want, then you are giving up control in determining your results or outcome. You are giving that person power and rendering yourself powerless.

9. **Willingness and Sacrifice:** You must be willing to do the things today in order to have the things tomorrow that others won't have.

10. **Perseverance:** Never give up. Quitters always quit, and winners always win. You never know how close you are to your win, so don't give in.

There's so much hidden potential on the inside of you. You are stars, so live your life accordingly in all areas. When you believe, anything's possible.

RESOURCES

I offer additional information to inspire you and your family on my website. Find information on inspiring your family at http://mooreofrachel.com/inspire/inspire-my-family/. For more details on Family Visioning Planning and Vision Board Party planning, visit http://mindyourvision.com.

Tote-a-Vision details: Get your Tote-a-Vision – Portable Vision Board at http://mooreofrachel.com. Give the gift of organization and achievement to someone you love. The Tote-a-Vision is a great gift for everyone in the family. It neatly organizes a place for the vision board and a notebook to capture your dreams and goals.

It is a portable vision board that gives you the ability to carry your goals both in written and in a visual form wherever you go. Up to three custom sized boards can fit comfortably in the body pocket at one time.

The Tote-a-Vision is a clear vinyl sleeve with a large pocket opening on the top edge to insert your vision boards. It includes a custom-sized white poster board, journal and how-to diagram. Refer to the website links for instructions on how to create a portable vision board, as well as get ideas on the different themes to consider for your vision boards.

Benefits of Tote-a-Vision:
- Portable and easy to carry visual representation of your vision, dreams, and goals

- Provides protection for your vision/dream boards inside clear vinyl protective sleeve
- Carry it with you and reflect on your vision daily
- Vinyl sleeve fits around a traditional composition notebook as a book cover. Your vision board becomes the cover of your journal and your personal inspiration
- Track goals, ideas, milestones, and achievements inside your journal
- Easy to interchange different vision boards

"Manifest More" Audio Course: If you want to accelerate your results even more, the *Manifest More* six-part audio course may interest you. Learn more at: https://mooreofrachel.com/manifest-more-program/

One of the most unique modules within this audio course is about "Hitting the Sweet Spot." It teaches how to recognize signs of Divine guidance which helps you navigate your actions precisely. The course also provides methods to give yourself a super solid mindset to conquer doubts that beset you. More benefits and course details can be found online.

Podcasts: Listen to me teach "The Wisdom Effect": http://www.womensradio.com/2016/04/the-wisdom-effect-part-1/ and part-2. Other Inside Out Empowerment podcasts can be found here: https://mooreofrachel.audioacrobat.com/rss/inside_out_empowerment.xml

Visit our Vision Board Gallery for Tote-a-Vision Board Examples at https://mindyourvision.com/gallery/

WORKS CITED

Di Stefano, Giada and Gino, Francesca and Pisano, Gary and Staats, Bradley R., Making Experience Count: The Role of Reflection in Individual Learning (June 14, 2016). Harvard Business School NOM Unit Working Paper No. 14-093; Harvard Business School Technology & Operations Mgt. Unit Working Paper No. 14-093; HEC Paris Research Paper No. SPE-2016-1181. Available at SSRN: https://ssrn.com/abstract=2414478 or http://dx.doi.org/10.2139/ssrn.2414478

The original acronym for SMART first appeared in the November 1981 issue of *Management Review*. "There's a S.M.A.R.T. way to write management goals and objectives" was the title, and it was written by George Doran, Arthur Miller, and James Cunningham. https://www.smart-goals-guide.com/smart-goal.html

MerriamWebster.com. "Ability," "Potential," and "Propagation." Accessed Feb. 2020.

Psychology Today. "Emotional Intelligence." https://www.psychologytoday.com/us/basics/emotional-intelligence. Accessed Feb. 2020.

Tanne, Richard, dir. *Southside with You*. 2016, Miramax. Theatrical release.

Zootopia. A 2016 American 3D computer-animated comedy film produced by Walt Disney Animation Studios and released by Walt Disney Pictures.

ABOUT THE AUTHOR

Rachel Moore is a daytime engineer and a nighttime entrepreneur. Rachel discovered purpose in helping others effectuate their dreams during her pursuit to create a fulfilled life for her family. Through her broad spectrum of experiences, as a wife, mom, engineer, inventor, author, and as a life empowerment coach, she provides products, training programs, and coaching to help bring clarity to your life vision. In 2017, Rachel became a *#1 international bestselling author* with her **Manager Mom: Mind Your Vision** book, which serves as an empowerment tool to women, teaching them how to live out their dreams while raising their children, or how to pursue their passions at any stage of life.

Those same mind-freeing techniques initially written to moms have been expanded into a more comprehensive solution to manifest more in your life. In this body of work, Rachel seeks to inspire and encourage anyone who has a desire, who has a vision, dream, or goal that has not yet been realized. In each story and example shared, you will be reminded that each day presents a new opportunity to believe for the possibilities as she tells how to create the life that you desire, even in the midst of undesirable circumstances. Her favorite motto is "Faith works when you work it."

As the CEO of Moore of Rachel, Inc., through visioning workshops, small group studies, home gatherings, and empowerment calls, she inspires not only women but also students of every age to achieve whatever they dream to be, do, or have. She seeks to inform, inspire, influence, and ignite others to appropriate action toward creating an incredibly fulfilled life of passion, purpose, abundance, freedom, and success.

Since 2009, Rachel has taught family visioning, individual dream-building, and team- building techniques within seminars and workshops in the USA and abroad, sharing examples of her own success and utilizing her US Patented portable vision board product called Tote-A-Vision to help attendees learn how to turn desires into dreams come true. Individuals, families, entrepreneurs, educators, students, and organizations have benefited from her proven success tools and techniques.

Rachel is a contributing author to the bestselling book series, Chicken Soup for the Soul - Say Goodbye to Stress book. As a member of The Professional Woman Network, she is a contributing author for their Getting Well: Mind, Body, & Spirit book. She is the author of Manager Mom - Mind Your Vision, and Rivers of Praise Worship through Movement, a comprehensive guide to worship. Some of her audio training programs are "Manifest More of My Dreams" and "CALM"— helping women to slow down the pace, relax, and care for themselves.

Rachel lives a low-carb lifestyle. She recently competed in the Ms. Health & Fitness Competition where she finished as a Semi-Finalist. In 2018, she won first place in the Bikini Masters in an INBF Southern Natural Body-Building Competition. Rachel shares recipes and fitness tips in her Low-Carb recipe books. She also offers programs to assist others with their fitness goals.

Rachel and Johnny, have four sons. She is the manager mom and mentor to her son's business pursuits.

Contact:

For more information, please visit www.mooreorachel.com
Email: rachel@mindyourvision.com
Facebook: www.Facebook.com/mindyourvison

www.ingramcontent.com/pod-product-compliance
Lightning Source LLC
Chambersburg PA
CBHW070544010526
44118CB00012B/1217